HV 8694 .I83 2003

Is the death penalty fair?

DATE DUE

NOV 29 03			
DEC 08 '04			
APR 0 4 '05			
FEB 28 '06			
DEC 15 '06			

IS THE DEATH PENALTY FAIR?

Mary E. Williams, *Book Editor*

Daniel Leone, *President*
Bonnie Szumski, *Publisher*
Scott Barbour, *Managing Editor*
Helen Cothran, *Senior Editor*

GREENHAVEN
PRESS ®

THOMSON
— ✳ —
GALE
THE EVANS LIBRARY-FMCC

San Diego • Detroit • New York • San Francisco • Cleveland
New Haven, Conn. • Waterville, Maine • London • Munich

For more information, contact
Greenhaven Press
27500 Drake Rd.
Farmington Hills, MI 48331-3535
Or you can visit our Internet site at http://www.gale.com

LIBRARY OF CONGRESS CATALOGING-IN-PUBLICATION DATA
Is the death penalty fair? / Mary E. Williams, book editor.
p. cm. — (At issue)
Includes bibliographical references and index.
ISBN 0-7377-1165-5 (pbk. : alk. paper) — ISBN 0-7377-1166-3 (lib. : alk. paper)
1. Capital punishment. I. Williams, Mary E., 1960– . II. At issue (San Diego, Calif.)
HV8694 .I83 2003
364.66—dc21   2002034656

Printed in the United States of America

Contents

Introduction

In the summer of 1984, a young girl was kidnapped, raped, and murdered near her home in Baltimore County, Maryland. Twenty-three-year-old Kirk Bloodsworth was accused of the crime, and he was convicted and sentenced to death after a jury trial based largely on the eyewitness testimony of some boys playing near the murder site.

Three days after Bloodsworth's conviction, police and prosecutors learned about David Rehill. Hours after the girl's murder, Rehill had shown up at a mental health clinic with fresh scratches on his face and had mentioned to therapists that he was "in trouble with a little girl." Rehill closely resembled Bloodsworth, who was already on death row. Six months passed before police decided to interview Rehill. Nevertheless, they did not place him in a lineup or doublecheck his alibi.

Due to a technical error in the trial, Bloodsworth was granted an appeal two years after his conviction. Even though prosecutors had known about Rehill for those two years, they withheld this information from the defense until two days before the second trial. Bloodsworth's attorneys did not have enough time to investigate the new information and failed to ask for a trial postponement. The second jury never learned that there was another suspect, and they also convicted Bloodsworth of rape and murder. In 1993, however, DNA analysis of the victim's clothing revealed that Bloodsworth could not have committed the crime, and he was exonerated. Trial observers and commentators were disquieted to learn that an innocent man had been sentenced to death.

Kirk Bloodsworth was not the first nor the last capital defendant to receive faulty legal representation, a death sentence, and eventual exoneration through postconviction evidence. In 1993, Gary Gauger was wrongfully convicted of murdering his parents on the basis of a coerced confession obtained by police after he was held for nearly twenty hours of questioning without food or access to an attorney. Gauger was acquitted only after a law professor took over the case and revealed solid information pointing to the real killers. In 2001, Earl Washington Jr. was released from prison after definitive DNA tests proved that he could not have committed the 1982 rape and murder that had led to his conviction and death sentence. An African American with an IQ indicating that he was retarded, Washington had allegedly "quickly" confessed to the crime even though he could not describe the victim or identify where or how he had killed her. Washington, Gauger, and Bloodsworth are among the more than ninety-five American death-row inmates who have been released from prison after charges against them were dropped due to wrongful convictions and overwhelming proof of innocence.

Americans' support of capital punishment, many death penalty critics contend, has been largely based on the assumption that only people who are undeniably guilty of felony murder are executed. However, for various reasons, innocent people can end up on death row. Faulty eyewitness identifications, false testimony—often presented by "jailhouse snitches" seeking reduced sentences—police misconduct, mishandled evidence, false confessions, inept legal representation, and the personal prejudices of jurors can lead to wrongful convictions.

Contributing to the occurrence of wrongful convictions is the problem of systemic discrimination based on race, class, or social status, many analysts maintain. According to death penalty opponents, the wrongly convicted are often "outsiders"—racial minorities, nonconformists, the poor, the mentally ill, or the mildly retarded—who do not receive equitable treatment in the criminal justice system. The mentally incompetent and the poor, in particular, cannot afford their own legal representation and are assigned court-appointed lawyers who are often overworked, inexperienced, or underpaid. Such scenarios make indigent defendants doubly vulnerable in cases in which police or prosecutors have suppressed evidence, critics point out. As Richard Dieter, executive director of the Death Penalty Information Center, states, "There is much that remains arbitrary and unfair about the death penalty."

As a result of the widely publicized stories about innocents on death row, American opinion on the death penalty has shifted. While a majority still support capital punishment, 80 percent of Americans also believe that an innocent person has been executed since 1995, and 63 percent support a suspension of executions until the fairness of capital trials can be determined. Reflecting this growing skepticism about the accuracy of murder convictions, Illinois governor George Ryan proclaimed a temporary moratorium on executions in his state in January 2000. Although he generally supports the death penalty, Ryan became alarmed when he learned that more than half of the condemned inmates in Illinois had been found innocent long after their convictions. In his announcement of the moratorium, Ryan stated, "I cannot support a system which, in its administration, has proven so fraught with error and has come so close to the ultimate nightmare, the state's taking of innocent life." In 2003, Ryan went one step further: He commuted his state's death sentences to sentences of life without parole.

Many death penalty critics agree with Ryan, arguing that the best way to ensure the protection of innocents is to replace the death penalty with the sentence of life in prison with no possibility of parole. But death penalty supporters often contend that concerns about executing innocents are mainly the result of biased media coverage. According to attorney Paul Kamenar, there have actually been "very few" cases involving the overturn of a death sentence, and "no case in the last 50 years where an innocent person was executed." He insists that "the death penalty is working and is working apparently at 100 percent accuracy."

Even the fact that death-sentence reversals have occurred, capital punishment supporters point out, reveals the adequacy of existing safeguards against arbitrary mistakes in death penalty cases. For one thing, there is an average of twelve years between conviction and execution, enough time to allow for several appeals. In addition, technological innovations, such as DNA testing, have greatly improved the quality of evidence collection at crime scenes, allowing for more accurate identification of suspects as well as providing exonerating evidence for those who have been wrongly accused.

But death penalty critics maintain that there will never be enough appeals or enough technology to absolve all innocent death-row inmates. As commentator Richard Cohen argues, human error will always be a factor in criminal investigations—which should be enough reason to abolish capital punishment: "To play God . . . in the face of all we know about human error is an expression of titanic arrogance coupled with a casual indifference to human life. . . . You can DNA test to your heart's content, provide money for crackerjack lawyers, look every prosecutor in the eye and make him cross his heart, but the innocent will, inevitably and with certainty, die anyway."

Many death penalty advocates, however, do not agree that unfairness in the administration of the death penalty nor the possibility of executing innocents justifies abolishing capital punishment. Some argue that the deterrent effect of the death penalty protects a greater number of innocents than are likely to be lost through wrongful executions. West Point teacher Louis Pojman maintains, for example, that "society has a right to protect itself from capital offenses even if this means taking a finite chance of executing an innocent person." Pojman offers compelling analogies to support his argument: "Fire trucks occasionally kill innocent pedestrians while racing to fires, but we accept these losses as justified by the greater good of the activity of using fire trucks. We judge the use of automobiles to be acceptable even though such use causes an average of 50,000 traffic fatalities each year. We accept the morality of a defensive war even though it will result in our troops accidentally or mistakenly killing innocent people." Unfairness and human fallibility will always exist, death penalty supporters contend, but they should not become obstacles to effective and just forms of punishment.

The recent debate about innocents on death row is likely to remain contentious in the years to come as more states consider legislation that would impose a moratorium on executions. The authors in *At Issue: Is the Death Penalty Fair?* present various opinions on the fairness of the death penalty and whether reforms can help prevent or reduce the possibility of wrongful executions.

1

The Death Penalty Is Unfair to Minorities and the Poor

Jeffery L. Johnson and Colleen F. Johnson

Philosophy professor Jeffery L. Johnson and economics professor Colleen F. Johnson both teach in the Philosophy, Politics, and Economics Department at Eastern Oregon University in La Grande, Oregon.

Socioeconomic discrimination is evident in the administration of the death penalty. Poor people and minorities are more likely than wealthy people to be convicted of crimes and to receive death sentences. Such disparities occur because poor defendants are generally represented by court-appointed attorneys who are often overworked, underpaid, inexperienced—or even incompetent. Prosecutors are also more likely to seek the death penalty in cases involving poor defendants because they realize that they are more likely to win such cases. In addition, the death penalty is more often pursued in cases involving wealthy or white murder victims. Until fair application of the death penalty can be guaranteed, individuals convicted of murder should be sentenced to life in prison without parole.

Disparities of wealth are inevitable within capitalism. Perhaps nowhere are these disparities more disturbing and deadly than in our system of justice and, in particular, in the way in which the death penalty is meted out in the United States. Our thesis is a simple one: Capital punishment in the United States is administered in an economically discriminatory way. The wealth disparity between those murderers who live and those who die constitutes a serious constitutional challenge to the permissibility of the death penalty. Our argument is not that we should somehow pity the vicious first degree murderer because of his economic misfortune, or in any way excuse or mitigate the moral and legal gravity of his offense, but rather that the most severe and solemn form of criminal punishment must be administered in a more economically even-handed way in order for any of us to take comfort in believing that justice was served by the murderer's death at the hands of the state. Our

Jeffery L. Johnson and Colleen F. Johnson, "Poverty and the Death Penalty," *Journal of Economic Issues*, vol. 35, June 2001, pp. 517–22. Copyright © 2001 by the Association for Evolutionary Economics. Reproduced by permission.

failure as a society to ensure some semblance of economic equality in our harshest criminal punishment constitutes a kind of procedural cruelty that is inconsistent with the Eighth Amendment to our Constitution. Unfortunately, our Supreme Court has demonstrated an almost pathological reticence to consider issues of class and wealth.

Contingent realities

We employ a strategy that might be called an "argument from contingent realities." We grant that moral, legal, or constitutional rules might sanction some practice in a more perfect (just, fair, equitable, etc.) world, but argue that given the contingent realities of the actual world, the practice in question is not to be permitted. That is, in the abstract capital punishment may not be unconstitutional, but in fact the way in which it is dispensed, we believe, puts it at odds with the Eighth Amendment and the Equal Protection Clause.

Capital punishment in the United States is administered in an economically discriminatory way.

Our Supreme Court seemed to have employed something like the contingent realities strategy in its very famous and controversial 1972 decision in *Furman v. Georgia*.[1] They were concerned that there seemed to be no rational link between the most serious murders and the death sentences imposed in individual trials. One could easily find cases in which equally brutal murders resulted in a death sentence in one trial and in a prison sentence in another. Indeed, it was relatively easy to find cases in which a much more atrocious murder resulted in prison when compared with another murder that resulted in a death sentence. Justice Potter Stewart used the helpful analogy of being struck by lightning to illustrate the contingent reality of rape and murder trials in the 1960s.

Since the Court saw the arbitrariness and capriciousness of capital punishment to be a direct function of unfettered jury discretion, the state of Georgia, in what became a model for the other states, set about to correct the problem. They first more narrowly defined the crime of aggravated first-degree murder. In addition they mandated a scheme of bifurcated trials—the first phase in which the jury determines factual guilt or innocence, and the second phase devoted to the jury's consideration of "aggravating" and "mitigating" circumstances that bear on the appropriateness of death. And finally they instituted automatic appellate review of all death sentences. In its pivotal 1976 decision in *Gregg v. Georgia* our Supreme Court ruled that "the statutory system under which Gregg was sentenced to death does not violate the Constitution."[2]

We believe that a quarter century's experience with the post-*Furman* death penalty procedures is an embarrassing constitutional failure. The

1. With this case, the Supreme Court temporarily abolished the death penalty, declaring that it had been applied arbitrarily and used unfairly against minorities and the poor.   2. This case reinstated the death penalty and created guidelines for determining whether a convicted criminal should receive a death sentence.

apparent caprice and unfairness in our application of state-sponsored death is every bit as prevalent as it was before 1972. There are at least two independent reasons for this.

The first is jurisprudential. In a series of decisions in the 1970s the Court mandated the following two constitutional directives:

1. "[T]he Eighth and Fourteenth Amendments cannot tolerate the infliction of death under legal systems that permit this unique penalty to be so wantonly and freakishly imposed" (*Furman v. Georgia*).

2. "[T]he fundamental respect for humanity underlying the Eighth Amendment . . . requires consideration of the character and record of the individual offender and the circumstances of the particular offense as a constitutionally indispensable part of the process of inflicting the death penalty" (*Woodson v. North Carolina*).

Principle 1 tells juries that they may not capriciously exercise their discretion in inflicting death as they see fit. Principle 2, however, may well force them to do precisely this. How can they possibly consider "the character and record of the individual offender," or "the circumstances of the particular offense," without exercising unlimited discretion to administer death on a case-by-case basis?

Disguised discrimination

A second, far greater source of caprice exists within the power of local prosecutors to determine which murders to prosecute as capital cases in the first place. Different moral and criminological philosophies, reelection concerns, media attention, and a host of other variables virtually guarantee that considerations beyond simple calculations of . . . seriousness will enter into a prosecutor's decision to seek the death penalty or not.

Our criminal justice system . . . is infected by prejudice and discrimination.

It is morally and constitutionally problematic to suppose that judges, juries, and prosecutors wield discretion over life and death in such a capricious manner. It is even more troublesome, however, if what appears to be arbitrary administration is really disguised bias and discrimination. We believe that capital punishment is not "freakish," but insidious. We would oppose the death penalty, were it simply a crap shoot, but this game is played with clearly loaded dice. Our criminal justice system, like every other institution in American society, is infected by prejudice and discrimination.

Since blacks are three times as likely to be poor as whites, it seems reasonable that race could serve to measure the impact of poverty on criminal charges, convictions, and sentencing. According to Michael Katz,

> In 1978, 53 percent of black jail inmates had pre-arrest incomes below $3,000, compared with 44 percent of whites.
> In 1983, the median pre-arrest income of black jail inmates

was $4,067 and that of white jail inmates was $6,312. About half of blacks in jail were unemployed before arrest and 44 percent of whites were.

For our purposes, evidence of racism will be treated as evidence of class bias.

In the area of arrests and charges, there is ample evidence of both racism and economic bias. Maynard L. Erikson argued that poor individuals from juveniles to adults are more likely to be arrested and charged than middle and upper-income individuals. Terence P. Thornberry found that juveniles from lower class families were more likely to be sent to juvenile court and less likely to receive probation than those from affluent homes.

The poor person is more likely to be found guilty of . . . crimes than is the wealthier defendant.

Theodore Chiricos et al. argued that the poor person is more likely to be found guilty of similar crimes than is the wealthier defendant. In part this is explained by the fact that the poor are less likely to make bail and more likely to be represented by a public defender. The effect of being unable to post bail may bias the verdict toward guilty because the defendant is unable to substantially assist in his own defense. The effects of being represented by a public defender are more varied and complex. Since public defenders typically have large case loads and are salaried employees, there is less economic incentive to devote extensive time to research and pretrial motions, activities which would clearly increase the chances that the charges would be dismissed.

Bias in sentencing

The final phase of the criminal justice system is sentencing and here, just as in the other phases, there is evidence that the harshest penalties are reserved for blacks and the poor. J. Petersilia found

> "that blacks and Hispanics are less likely to be given probation, more likely to receive prison sentences, more likely to receive longer sentences, and more likely to serve a greater portion of their original time."

As with conviction rates, this may in part be due to blacks and the poor being more likely to be represented by public defenders. According to Stephen Bright,

> A court-appointed defense lawyer's only reference to his client during the penalty phase of a Georgia capital case was: "You have got a little ole nigger man over there that doesn't weigh over 135 pounds. He is poor and he is broke. He's got an appointed lawyer. . . . He is ignorant. I will venture to say he has an IQ of not over 80." The defendant was sentenced to death.

We all understand how historic and contemporary attitudes of racial prejudice could affect capital sentencing. It is less clear how a person's socioeconomic class could bias the outcome of a death penalty case to such a degree that it would implicate both the Equal Protection Clause and the Eighth Amendment. We want to suggest two interrelated ways in which a defendant's poverty could work to his—and in rare instances, her—disadvantage in the context of a capital sentence. In addition, we will speculate on a third factor involving the socioeconomic class, not of the defendant, but of the victim.

We vacillate in our commitment to neoclassical economic theory, but we concede the wisdom in the economic homily "you get what you pay for." The most obvious way that the current system works to the disadvantage of poor people is in the amount of professional compensation provided for indigent defense in capital cases. In the 1980s, Alabama put a limit of $1,000 on out-of-court compensation; attorneys in rural Texas received as little as $800 for a capital case; and Kentucky imposed an upper [limit] of $2,500. We assume that the amazing comment to the jury quoted above is only partially a result of incompetence and racism, but also the fact, as he went out of the way to tell the jury, that he was appointed by the court to represent the defendant. We have no record of how much he was compensated, but we can guess that it varied from the attorney's fees in the O.J. Simpson case by orders of magnitude.

The harshest penalties are reserved for blacks and the poor.

Stephen Bright aptly titled a recent article in *The Yale Law Journal* "Counsel for the Poor: The Death Sentence Not for the Worst Crime but for the Worst Lawyer." He chronicled, not with the nice statistical data that we wish we had but with anecdote after anecdote stories of drunken court-appointed attorneys, ones with no experience, grievous strategic errors, and gross ignorance of relevant law. The pattern here is so pervasive that these injustices should be addressed, not on the appeal of individual death sentences but in terms of the overall equality of the institution of capital punishment.

Other effects of poverty on the death penalty

Resource equity is also an issue with the other prevalent system for providing indigent defense. Public defenders' offices are not staffed by drunks, racists, or professionally incompetent attorneys. Indeed, they are usually bright, energetic, and highly dedicated professionals. The problem here is not salary or compensation, though being a public defender is certainly not a ticket to wealth and luxury, but one of excessive case loads. Again the story is most effectively told anecdotally, but perhaps a Louisiana Supreme Court ruling can serve as a summary. In *State v. Peart* the court ruled that excessive case loads and under-funding of such necessary ingredients of an adequate criminal defense as investigative support and expert witnesses amounted to a failure on Louisiana's part to "provide . . . the effective assistance of counsel the constitution requires."

There are two other ways poverty influences the death penalty—they occur long before cases are prosecuted in the criminal courts. Both have to do with decisions on the part of the state as to how to prosecute the defendant. Capital cases are incredibly high stakes occurrences, not just for the defendant but also for the state. Issues of prestige and credibility are raised, in the abstract for the state and in very personal terms for the district attorney. In addition, they are much more expensive to litigate. Consequently, the state chooses its capital cases very carefully. Huge factors are the odds of winning, the relative cost of the prosecution, and the degree of community pressure. Indigent defendants are relatively good bets for district attorneys considering the possibility of asking for the death penalty.

The second way that socioeconomic status is implicated in the death penalty can most easily be appreciated if we again use race as a proxy for wealth. Several studies have demonstrated that the race of the murder victim causally influences the decision whether to seek the death penalty. We take it to be obvious that the wealth of the victim is equally relevant. We are convinced that murder victims who are poor, regardless of their race, are afforded an unequal, second-class status.

Life without parole is preferable

If the preceding analysis is at all persuasive, fairly dramatic changes in our criminal justice system seem morally and constitutionally required. We would recommend that capital punishment be abandoned, at least until the contingent realities of this society are significantly altered and in its place federal and state statutes mandate a punishment of life imprisonment without the possibility of parole for the crime of aggravated murder. Many of our students seem to feel that such a punishment would be mere rhetoric and that these evil and dangerous individuals would soon be on the streets. In point of fact, however, the sentence is just what it says, and it has withstood court challenges.

The threat of spending the rest of one's life in a maximum security prison acts as a very strong negative incentive to aggravated murder. Whether this threat would be as effective as death in deterring these horrible crimes is still a matter of some controversy among social scientists— economists tend to insist that theory mandates that capital punishment must be a more effective deterrent, while criminologists despair any reliable data to support such an hypothesis. All parties would agree, however, that any differentials are extremely slight and, by implication, that life imprisonment is an effective deterrent.

Most candidates for capital punishment are extremely violent and dangerous individuals who should not be at large in society. Life imprisonment without parole guarantees that we need not fear that they will repeat their crimes. Skeptics will argue, of course, that there remain dangers of escape or of murders committed while in prison. Such occurrences are possible. But life without parole forecloses the possibility of aggravated murderers being intentionally released, and this, after all, is the major public safety concern.

Part of our moral and political justification for criminal punishment is retributive. Most of us believe that criminals have unfairly taken advantage of the rest of us and that abstract standards of justice demand that they "pay back" society for their crimes when they are legally convicted. The most serious crimes "deserve" the most serious punishment. Life without parole would be society's harshest criminal punishment. It would be reserved for those truly horrible crimes for which justice demands the "ultimate" penalty.

One argument against capital punishment that seems to resonate with everyday citizens is that there is a risk of executing individuals who are innocent of the crimes for which they were convicted. We believe that the danger is real and that the preceding analysis explains a big part of it. When capital defendants are represented by inexperienced, underpaid, and in some cases incompetent, attorneys, it should come as no surprise that legal and strategic mistakes are common. We can only feel confident that the truly guilty are the ones being executed when everyone is afforded the same quality (and quantity) of criminal defense. Since we all know that the contingent realities of this world preclude such equal advocacy, and since most of us acknowledge that risk of executing the innocent is profound, life without parole eliminates the risk, though sadly does not address the issue of wrongful convictions that result in prison sentences.

2

The Death Penalty Is Not Unfair to Blacks

John McAdams

John McAdams is a professor of political science at Marquette University.

The argument that the death penalty should be abolished because it is unfair—particularly that it is applied in a racially biased manner—is illogical. On the one hand, death penalty opponents contend that African Americans are more likely than whites to receive death sentences. On the other hand, these critics also argue that murderers of blacks are treated more leniently than murderers of whites. However, since the vast majority of homicides involve perpetrators and victims of the same race, it is generally blacks who are convicted for murdering blacks. Therefore, the claim that killers of blacks are treated more leniently contradicts the argument that blacks are overrepresented on death row. The truth is that widespread discrimination is not evident in the application of capital punishment. The death penalty is administered as fairly as other public policies are, and it should be retained.

W e should, generically, want fairness in all areas of public policy. And we should especially want fairness with regard to the death penalty, since the stakes are high. But the opponents of the death penalty make a most peculiar argument about fairness. They argue that if the death penalty is not administered fairly, and especially [not] administered with racial fairness, it must be abolished.

Nobody would even think of trying to apply this principle in a consistent way. If we find that black neighborhoods get less police protection than white neighborhoods, would we withdraw cops from both black and white neighborhoods? If banks are discriminating against black home buyers in mortgage lending, would we demand they stop all mortgage lending? If we find the IRS discriminating against middle-class and poor taxpayers, would we want to abolish the IRS? All right, that does have an attraction, but nobody is seriously suggesting it.

What do the opponents of the death penalty say should replace it? Life imprisonment, perhaps? But there is no reason to believe this penalty

John McAdams, "Yes: Can the Death Penalty Be Administered Fairly?" *Spectrum: The Journal of State Government*, vol. 71, Winter 1998, pp. 28–29. Copyright © 1998 by the Council of State Governments. Reproduced by permission.

is more fairly imposed than the death penalty. So are we going to knock the maximum down to 10 years? If so, we face the same problem.

In addition to the philosophical incoherence of the argument, the empirical reality of racial disparity in capital punishment is a lot more complicated than simplistic notions about racism run riot in the criminal justice system would lead you to believe. It's important here to understand that the opponents of the death penalty make two different arguments about racial fairness, and they are flatly contradictory.

The first thing that we see when we start looking at statistics is that blacks are over represented on death row. Thus, we might conclude that the system is unfairly harsh on black defendants. Many have. As Frank Chapman said: "For 48 percent of the death row population in our country to be black is clearly practicing genocide when you consider that Afro-Americans are only 12 percent of the population." Somewhat more recent figures show 41.7 percent of the death row population to be black, and of all prisoners executed since 1988, 38.7 percent have been black. Presumably, this is because of racist prejudice against black defendants on the part of prosecutors, or juries, or on the part of the voting public to which judges and prosecutors are responsible in a democracy.

I call this the mass market version of the racial disparity argument.

But then suppose we look a bit further. Notice that 48 percent of murder victims are black (in 1995). And then we notice that the vast majority of murders are intraracial and not interracial. Among murders involving blacks and whites, 90 percent involve a white killing a white or a black killing a black. Almost three-quarters of the rest involve blacks murdering whites, and only a small handful involve whites murdering blacks. Knowing this, the number of blacks on death row, and the number of blacks executed doesn't look far out of line.

Hard statistical evidence fails to support the politically correct fantasy of massive discrimination.

But we want to go beyond eyeballing numbers to get a solid assessment of bias. To do that, we have to control for factors that might legitimately result in more or less severe sentences. The opponents of the death penalty have actually cited the fact that blacks who murder whites are treated more harshly than blacks who murder blacks to argue for racial bias in the system. Unfortunately, the odds of black on white murders being comparable to black on black murders are about zero.

White on black murders are rare, and difficult to deal with statistically, so what we are basically left with is a comparison of the treatment of blacks who murder blacks, and whites who murder whites.

And what do we find when we make this comparison? As scholars such as Gary Kleck, William J. Bowers, Sheldon Ekland-Olson and David Baldus have shown, murderers of blacks who are themselves overwhelmingly black are treated more leniently than murderers of whites. Of course, this can be formulated in a politically correct manner, as a bias against black victims. As Randall L. Kennedy, describing David Baldus' study, remarked: In the marketplace of emotion, the lives of blacks simply count for less than the lives of whites.

I call this the specialist version of the racial disparity argument. I'm quite happy with this formulation, since it expresses concern for the victims of crime. But I can't avoid noticing that it flatly contradicts the mass market version.

What the data reveal

But given that racial disparity is real, how severe is it? David Baldus, who is probably the top scholar in the area, recently described the statistical findings:

> . . . what do the data tell us about differences in discrimination in the pre- and post-*Furman* periods [after legislatures tightened sentencing procedures in response to the court's ruling]? There are significant differences in race effects, both across and within states. There are differences in the magnitude of race effects at different decision-making levels in the states i.e., prosecutorial decisions to seek the death penalty and jury decisions to impose death. There are also differences that correlate with culpability. The risk of race effects was very low in the most aggravated capital cases; however, in the mid-range cases, where the correct sentence was less clear, and the room for exercise of discretion much broader, the race disparities are much stronger. Whereas the overall average disparity for the two groups (black v. white) tends to be 6–8 percentage points, in the mid-range cases the disparities are typically two to three times that large [12 to 24 percentage points].

Baldus then goes on to describe some reactions to his findings:

> There is much anecdotal evidence from lawyers who represent capital defendants. Many of them seriously question the validity of statistical studies that do not reveal disparities based upon the race of the defendant. It is possible that there is such discrimination, but that it is not sufficiently large and systematic to be picked up by the data.

Baldus, perhaps out of politeness, doesn't note that lawyers are in the business of producing anecdotal evidence to support their client's position, and that those who represent capital defendants are a highly self-selected and hardly unbiased group.

So what we have, in the way of hard statistical evidence, fails to support the politically correct fantasy of massive discrimination. Is the death penalty administered with perfect fairness? No. Is it administered as fairly as other public policies, and especially as fairly as other criminal sanctions? Yes.

Public officials should work to make the system even fairer. In particular, better provision could be made for an effective defense in capital cases. And I think that a revival of executive clemency (which has fallen into disuse) in cases where a jury is perceived to have been too harsh would be a good thing. But the notion that unfairness, and particularly racial unfairness, requires the end of the death penalty makes neither philosophical nor empirical sense.

3

Executing the Mentally Retarded Is Unfair

Human Rights Watch

Human Rights Watch is a private nonprofit organization that promotes respect for internationally recognized civil and political rights.

By law, murder suspects who are found to be mentally incompetent are not subjected to court trials that could lead to a death sentence. However, declarations of mental incompetence are rare, and many mentally retarded suspects have been tried for murder and sentenced to death. Allowing the mentally retarded to face charges of homicide and trials that could result in execution is patently unfair. Their disabilities render them especially vulnerable to exploitation, neglect, and flawed criminal justice procedures. Some mentally retarded people, for example, want to please authority figures and will eagerly confess to crimes they did not commit. These false confessions, along with the oftentimes inadequate legal representation the mentally retarded receive, increase the chances that innocents will be put to death.

The prosecution and trial of capital defendants in the United States is notoriously flawed by arbitrariness, prejudice, and error. These flaws are magnified when the defendant has mental retardation. By virtue of their disability, people with mental retardation are even less likely than other defendants to be able to protect their legal rights and to secure a fair trial. Even before they run afoul of the law, the intellectual and adaptive deficits of mentally retarded people render them uniquely vulnerable to abuse and exploitation. These vulnerabilities continue to haunt them once they are enmeshed in the criminal justice system.

If a person is so profoundly retarded as to be deemed mentally incompetent he or she will not be required to stand trial. In practice, however, findings of mental incompetence are extremely rare. Once adjudicated as competent to stand trial, a person with mental retardation is deemed capable of understanding the nature and purpose of the legal proceedings and of cooperating, communicating and working with defense counsel. The law does not require specially designed aids or procedures to assist the "mentally competent" person suffering from retardation. Yet even people with less severe degrees of retardation are significantly impaired in their ability to understand and protect their rights and to assist in their own defense.

For example, one attribute of mental retardation is the inability to reason abstractly and to comprehend abstract concepts—including the most basic concepts relevant to criminal proceedings. Robert Wayne Sawyer—an offender with mental retardation executed in 1993—was asked by a psychiatrist interviewing him to define "evidence." "It's what lawyers put on a yellow pad like the one you're using," was the best definition Sawyer could offer. When asked what "reasonable doubt" meant, Sawyer put out his cigarette, pointed to the residual smoke and said, "That smoke ain't reasonable out, but when it stops, it's reasonable out." When asked if he could provide an explanation that did not involve a cigarette, Sawyer said he could not.

Waiver of rights

At various stages in the proceedings against them, criminal suspects face important decisions about whether to waive their constitutional and statutory rights, e.g. the right to refrain from answering police questions, and the right to a trial by jury. Before giving effect to such waivers, the courts are obliged to determine, based on the totality of the circumstances, whether the waiver was voluntary and made with full awareness of the nature of the right being waived and the consequences of the decision to waive it. The courts, however, frequently accept waivers by people with mental retardation without sufficient regard for the nature of the disability and its impact on such crucial decisions. Many people with mental retardation relinquish critical rights simply because they cannot understand what it means to have a "right," much less what it means to waive it. As reported in a 1999 Human Rights Watch interview with Clive Stafford-Smith, executive director of the Louisiana Crisis Assistance Center: "Eddie Mitchell, a retarded man on death row in Louisiana, waived all his rights during his interrogation. But when an attorney asked him if he had understood what "waiving his rights" meant, Mitchell raised his right hand and waved."

> *[The] mentally incompetent . . . [are not] required to stand trial. In practice, however, findings of mental incompetence are extremely rare.*

The right against self-incrimination—either during interrogation or trial—is protected by the Fifth Amendment to the U.S. Constitution and is recognized as a basic human right by the International Covenant on Civil and Political Rights. The importance of this right cannot be overemphasized, as a confession almost invariably results in a conviction, even without corroborating evidence. To protect the right against self-incrimination, confessions made during police interrogations cannot be admitted into evidence at trial unless the police have given a "Miranda warning," informing the suspects of the right to remain silent, to have an attorney present and that anything said could be used against them. A suspect may waive these rights, but the waiver is invalid unless it is "knowing, intelligent and voluntary."

People with mental retardation almost invariably waive their "Miranda" rights and confess to the police without the presence of counsel. Their waivers are necessarily suspect given the characteristics of their disability.

"Some of the retarded are characterized by a desire to please authority: if a confession will please, it will be gladly given."

People with mental retardation will ordinarily lack the intellectual capacity to make an informed decision regarding whether to confess without the presence of counsel. Mental retardation often means the defendant cannot understand the seriousness of the situation, cannot identify and assess the ramifications of a confession, and lacks the ability even to understand that he has an option of whether or not to confess. Indeed, a person with even mild retardation may not comprehend the vocabulary used in the standard Miranda warning or the abstract concepts that it embodies. Miranda warnings are written at a seventh-grade level of difficulty; many people with mental retardation in the criminal justice system function at a lower intellectual level and are unable to understand the language and meanings of the warning. As James Ellis and Ruth Luckasson, leading experts on mental retardation and the criminal justice system, have noted:

> The concepts of what "rights" are, what it means to give them up voluntarily, the notion of the ability to refuse to answer questions asked by a person of great authority, the concept of the subsequent use of incriminating statements, the right to counsel and the right to have the state pay for that counsel, and the idea that the suspect can delay answering questions until a lawyer arrives are all of some abstraction and difficulty. A substantial number of retarded people will not know what one or more of these ideas means. A related difficulty is that the vocabulary of many retarded people is so limited; they may not be able to understand the warning even if they are familiar with its component concepts.

A careful inquiry is needed to determine whether a person with mental retardation does, in fact, comprehend the nature and significance of a waiver of rights. Yet, the police and the courts frequently limit themselves to seeking yes-or-no answers to questions that are themselves abstract—e.g. asking whether the suspect understands his rights and is willing to waive them. According to Paul T. Hourihan:

Earl Washington waived his Miranda rights and confessed to a murder he did not commit. On appeal, his lawyers challenged the admissibility of his confession, arguing, *inter alia,* that it was not made "knowingly" because of Washington's mental retardation. The Virginia Supreme Court rejected Washington's appeal, in part because it believed that a series of "yes sir" responses when Washington was asked if he knew he was waiving his constitutional rights provided "clear indications" of his understanding. When asked specific questions during trial about his understanding of the contents of the waiver, however, it was clear that Washington did not understand what he had signed; indeed, he was not even aware of the meaning of some of the words used in the form.

If the nature and meaning of the Miranda warning are carefully, simply, and clearly explained, some people with retardation may be able to understand it. In practice, however, it is rare for police to do anything other than recite the standard warning. One state court suggested the following general rule: "When expert testimony indicates that a defendant could have intelligently understood the waiver of his constitutional rights only if they were simply and clearly explained, the record must expressly and specifically establish that such an explanation was given."

"Voluntariness"

The "voluntariness" of confessions by persons with mental retardation is also suspect. Such persons are susceptible to non-physical forms of coercion, pressure and intimidation by the police that people with normal intelligence can more readily withstand. They are less able to handle the stress and fear of a police interrogation, particularly if the questioning is prolonged. They are also less likely to resist the efforts of an apparently "friendly" police questioner. Their characteristic desire to please figures of authority can lead them to do whatever they think necessary to gain approval. It can be almost impossible for them to make a decision to remain silent in the face of police efforts to get them to talk.

Innocent people with mental retardation all too often confess to capital crimes they did not commit.

The Task Force on Law of the President's Panel on Mental Retardation warned decades ago, in 1963:

> [T]he retarded are particularly vulnerable to an atmosphere of threats and coercion, as well as to one of friendliness designed to induce confidence and cooperation. A retarded person may be hard put to distinguish between the fact and the appearance of friendliness. If his life has been molded into a pattern of submissiveness, he will be less able than the average person to withstand normal police pressures. . . .

> Some of the retarded are characterized by a desire to please authority: if a confession will please, it will be gladly given. . . . It is unlikely that the retarded will see the implications or consequences of his statements in the way a person of normal intelligence will.

Traditionally, in assessing the voluntariness of a confession, the U.S. courts have considered the totality of the circumstances, including both objective factors—the conduct of police during an interrogation—and subjective factors, such as the intellectual and emotional characteristics of the suspect. The presence of mental retardation is clearly relevant to the voluntariness inquiry. However, in 1986, in *Colorado v. Connelly,* the U.S. Supreme Court issued a ruling that has been widely interpreted to require proof of official coercion, objectively defined, as a prerequisite to a determination that a waiver of rights and a confession were involuntary. As a result, most federal courts refuse to find a confession invalid simply because a defendant was affected by internal pressures or compulsions which were not a product of objective coercion, or because the defendant was unusually susceptible to psychological pressure. Such an approach effectively discounts the special needs of defendants with mental retardation and fails to provide adequate protection to suspects who, even absent police misconduct, are easily led into making incriminating statements.

The rights of persons with mental retardation would be best protected if no waiver could be provided or confession given absent the presence of a lawyer for the suspect. Indeed, the explanation of the Miranda warning should be provided by the lawyer so that the suspect with mental retardation is not implicitly induced by an apparently concerned and friendly officer into waiving his or her rights. U.S. courts, however, have not insisted on such a requirement.

False confessions

Innocent people with mental retardation all too often confess to capital crimes they did not commit, simply because they want to give the "right" answer to a police officer, or because they believe that if the police say they did something, they must have done it, even if they do not remember. In a legal system that gives enormous weight to confessions, even when they are uncorroborated by other evidence, the vulnerability, suggestibility, and eagerness to please of mentally retarded people can place their lives at risk.

Police in the United States are able to use virtually any method short of physical force to obtain a confession from a criminal suspect. They can lie, for instance, falsely claiming that they possess evidence they lack; they can shout angrily and make threats; they can wear a suspect down through bullying and prolonged interrogations. Such tactics can be difficult to withstand, even for people with normal intelligence who are innocent. Numerous suspects with mental retardation . . . have confessed falsely to capital crimes that were in fact committed by others.

People with mental retardation often try to compensate for their mental and developmental deficits by saying and doing whatever they think will please authority figures—and they are often highly attuned to the subtle and even not-so-subtle clues their interlocutors may give about what constitutes "the right answer" to a given question. Mentally retarded people may end up making false confessions that the police believe because the confessions contain details that "only the criminal could have known." The details, however, come from the police. Consider, for instance, this excerpt from the police interrogation of David Vasquez, a Virginia man with mental retardation, who confessed to a crime he did not commit.

Detective 1: Did she tell you to tie her hands behind her back?

Vasquez: Ah, if she did, I did.

Detective 2: Whatcha use?

Vasquez: The ropes?

Detective 2: No, not the ropes. Whatcha use?

Vasquez: Only my belt.

Detective 2: No, not your belt. . . . Remember being out in the sun room, the room that sits out to the back of the house? . . . and what did you cut down? To use?

Vasquez: That, uh, clothesline?

Detective 2: No, it wasn't a clothesline, it was something like a clothesline. What was it? By the window? . . . Think about the venetian blinds, David. Remember cutting the venetian blind cords?

Vasquez: Ah, it's the same as rope.

Detective 2: Yeah.

. . .

Detective 1: Okay, now tell us how it went, David—tell us how you did it.

Vasquez: She told me to grab the knife, and, and, stab her, that's all.

Detective 2: (voice raised) David, no, David.

Vasquez: If it did happen, and I did it, and my fingerprints were on it. . . .

Detective 2: (slamming his hand on the table and yelling) You hung her!

Vasquez: What?

Detective 2: You hung her!

Vasquez: Okay, so I hung her. . . .

After confessing, David Vasquez was charged with capital murder in February, 1984. He pled guilty to second-degree murder to avoid the death penalty and received a sentence of thirty-five years for murder and burglary. He was pardoned in 1989 when the true murderer was finally discovered.

Not only can the police be fooled by a false confession from a retarded defendant, but the defendant himself can be fooled. When police deliberately or unconsciously supply crucial details to a suspect with mental retardation, causing him to "confess," he may come to believe his own false confession—especially after repeating it several times to authority figures who validate its truth. Scharlette Holdman, a mitigation specialist who works for criminal defendants with mental retardation, noted: "After a confession, the person with mental retardation's memory is contaminated by the police, so you never get at the reality of what events transpired."

Ineffective assistance of counsel

It is well documented that many capital defendants receive inadequate counsel, often because courts appoint attorneys for the indigent who are too inexperienced, overworked, or uninterested to do an effective job. As a result, numerous death penalty cases are marred by serious errors: a recent comprehensive examination of thousands of death penalty cases during the past three decades, undertaken by Columbia University professors at the request of the chair of the Senate Judiciary Committee, found that appeals courts identified prejudicial, reversible errors in sixty-eight percent of all capital cases they reviewed. Aside from deliberate police or prosecutorial misconduct (e.g., withholding exculpatory evidence), the most common cause of serious error in capital cases is "egregiously incompetent" defense lawyers. Similarly, the *Dallas Morning News* reported that of 461 death row inmates in Texas, fully one quarter had been represented by attorneys who had been reprimanded, placed on probation, suspended, or disbarred by the Texas Bar Association.

Not only can the police be fooled by a false confession from a retarded defendant, but the defendant himself can be fooled.

Effective assistance by trial counsel includes a thorough and diligent investigation into all matters relevant to the determination of guilt or innocence as well as to sentencing, e.g., into mitigating factors. Inadequate investigations for either phase can doom a client. So can a failure to act as a committed, conscientious advocate for the defendant's life when arguing his case to the jury. All too often, however, mentally retarded defendants are represented by trial attorneys who provide inadequate, even abysmal, representation. According to Emily F. Reed, author of *The Penry Penalty*:

> During the capital trial of Larry Jones, his lawyer did not present Jones's age at the time of the crime (seventeen) or his retardation (an I. Q. of 41 or lower) as mitigating factors. The lawyer also did not make any closing arguments, leaving

> Jones, who had the mental age of a three- to five-year-old, to present his own. Jones was found guilty and sentenced to death. Ultimately, a court found that Larry Jones had not received effective assistance of counsel: as the court stated, Jones's lawyer "presented no proof to the jury of [the] mitigating factors of age and mental disability. He presented no mitigating circumstances at all. When the prosecution rested, he rested. . . . Defense counsel either neglected or ignored critical matters of mitigation at the point when the jury was to decide whether to sentence Jones to death. . . . [T]his failure was professionally unreasonable, and it was prejudicial to the defendant in that there is a reasonable probability that had this evidence been presented, the jury would have concluded that death was not warranted."

Robert Sawyer, executed in Louisiana in 1993, was also represented by defense counsel who did nothing to prepare for the penalty phase of Sawyer's trial. For example, he made no effort to uncover—and hence never presented to the jury—readily available evidence that Sawyer was mentally retarded, had been adjudicated incompetent on two prior occasions, had severe organic brain damage, had been a patient in four mental health facilities, had been left motherless as an infant by his mother's suicide, and as a child suffered beatings by a father described as sadistic by other members of the family.

Robert Anthony Carter's lawyer made a closing statement at his trial that was largely unintelligible, unfocused, and contained remarkably prejudicial comments. He asked the jury to give Carter the consideration of life "even though he doesn't deserve a great deal of consideration." He also told the jury that they could go either way in this case (i.e. grant life or the death penalty) "and your consciences would be clear." Although this lawyer acknowledged after the trial that Carter's childlike behavior possibly suggested some form of mental impairment, he had not attempted to obtain medical records for Carter or investigate his family history, nor did he request funds from the court for a psychological examination of Carter. Carter was, in fact, mentally retarded and seriously brain-damaged and had a childhood history of brutal physical abuse.

Sadly, these cases are not unique. The U.S. Supreme Court has ruled that every defendant has the right to receive "reasonably effective" counsel and is entitled to a new trial or sentencing procedure if the counsel's poor performance prejudiced his or her defense. But, in practice, many cases of ineffective assistance of counsel go unremedied. Courts, unfortunately, are reluctant to overturn sentences on the basis of poor lawyer performance. It is troubling enough that capital defendants can pay with their life for their counsel's failings; it is particularly intolerable that defendants with mental retardation who have no ability to evaluate their counsel's performance can pay the same price.

The special vulnerabilities of people with mental retardation make it critically important for them to have experienced, committed counsel. But these same vulnerabilities can make it harder for even the best of counsel to function effectively. Offenders with mental retardation often cannot assist their lawyers in preparing their defense as a defendant with normal intelligence could do. For example, people with mental retardation typically find it difficult to recall information that might help an attorney—in part because of problems with memory, in part because they are not able to conceptualize what information might be helpful. The trial lawyer for Johnny Paul Penry, for example, told Human Rights Watch that Penry was unable to answer open-ended questions about his activities on the day of the murder for which he was ultimately convicted. If asked leading questions, Penry would provide inconsistent yes or no responses depending on how the questions were formulated and what Penry apparently believed his attorney wanted him to say.

4

The Mentally Retarded Do Not Face Execution

Dudley Sharp

Dudley Sharp is the vice president of Justice for All, a Texas-based victims' rights group.

Those who argue against executing the mentally retarded are creating confusion about how the death penalty is applied. For decades, the legal system has not permitted the execution of the mentally retarded; only the mentally competent are allowed to be defendants in trials that could result in a death sentence or a prison term. Critics who contend that mentally retarded people have been executed are usually basing their claims on unreliable IQ evaluations. Mental competence should not be judged by IQ alone because intelligence can change over time. Moreover, competent criminals can intentionally score poorly on IQ tests in an attempt to evade execution. Courts should continue the practice of determining the defendant's mental competence before the case goes to trial.

Much of the presentation regarding excluding the execution of the mentally retarded has been either highly deceptive or lacking in a clinical foundation or both.

We hope this essay helps to correct that.

Some say that we mustn't execute people who do not know right from wrong and who lack understanding of the severity of their crimes. The reality is that we have not been executing such people for decades, because current law doesn't allow it.

Currently, during pre-trial, trial and appeals, the law provides evaluation for mental competency—and such an evaluation requires that the defendants understand the consequences of their actions, that they must be able to constructively participate in their own defense and that they understand the nature of their punishment. Furthermore, mental capability is one of the many issues that a jury might consider when establishing mitigation which may dictate a sentence less than death. Quite

Dudley Sharp, "Mental Retardation and the Death Penalty," www.prodeathpenalty.com, October 18, 2001. Copyright © 2001 by Justice for All. Reproduced by permission.

simply, only mentally competent capital murderers can face either execution or life in prison.

And that is appropriate.

Obfuscation and ignorance

Here is an example of the type of obfuscation and ignorance that is often seen within this issue.

Death penalty opponents state that Texas has executed 6 mentally retarded capital murderers. Those executed are defined as mentally retarded by their IQ numbers. First, mental health professions state that IQ measurements alone cannot establish mental retardation. So states that solely use that standard to exclude a possible death sentence have used an improper standard and these who declare people mentally retarded simply by IQ numbers are equally incorrect.

Those Texas six are called mentally retarded because they allegedly had a measured IQ of below 70—a standard below which some establish mental retardation. First, death penalty opponents will often list only the lowest recorded general IQ numbers of the murderer and intentionally withhold other tests which recorded much higher numbers. Such opponents also fail to note that there is a margin of error of plus or minus 10 points within that IQ evaluation, meaning that only those who score below a 60 on their maximum IQ test can establish mental retardation by using those numbers.

Furthermore, general IQ is not even relevant to the evaluations. Only performance IQ, which attempts to measure a person's abilities to function effectively under real world situations, is the relevant issue, if one improperly wishes to just 'go by the numbers'. Again, those states and advocates who use only general IQ evaluations have misunderstood or improperly applied that qualification.

Only mentally competent capital murderers can face either execution or life in prison.

And based on that analysis, as well as a review of the case facts, such opponents cannot support their claims that Texas has executed even a single mentally retarded murderer. I suggest that may likely be the case in other states, as well.

A case example:

During a Texas legislative session in the spring of 2001, supporters of HB236, a bill to ban execution of the mentally retarded, held a public rally at the capital in Austin and invoked the case of Mario Marquez, executed in 1995, as one of those 6 cases and stated that Marquez was exactly that kind of murderer which HB236 was designed to protect. Supporters of that bill could not have provided a better case for Texans to oppose this bill and for Governor Rick Perry to veto it.

Marquez was angry that his wife was leaving him, so, in retaliation, he murdered his wife's 14-year-old niece, Rachel, and his 18-year-old estranged wife, Rebecca. They were beaten and raped, orally, anally and vaginally, then strangled to death. Rebecca was sodomized with a large perfume bottle which was forced into her anus. Blood loss from both victims indicated that they were alive during these acts. Marquez then waited for his mother-in-law to return home, beat and sexually assaulted her—then presented the two brutalized bodies of the two girls to her—as trophies for his anger.

There is little doubt but that he was also going to murder his mother-in-law, but Marquez's continued assault on her was interrupted and he fled from the scene.

Marquez's performance IQ was measured at 75—16 points above the minimum number required to establish that arbitrary "mental retardation" standard, using the plus or minus 10 point variable. And Marquez's life and crimes, spanning many years, fully support that Marquez knew exactly what he was doing.

When given the facts of specific crimes, like Marquez's, many would agree with the jury—that such mentally competent, guilty capital murderers should face the death penalty, as a sentencing option.

Other considerations

There are some additional considerations:

1. Many argue strenuously to halt execution of the "mentally retarded", yet they do nothing to properly define what "mentally retarded" means in a fashion reflecting a full understanding of the issues, much less do they discuss the premeditation, planning, and consideration which the alleged "mentally retarded" murderers so often invested in the murders. A full accounting should be demanded in any public policy discussion, and

2. Many argue strenuously against a death penalty option for the mentally retarded, but they fail to tell us why such individuals should not be subject to execution, but should be subject to a life sentence. Is the murderer any less guilty or culpable for one sentence than the other? A jury may decide that the murderer deserves a lesser sentence, because of any mitigation which may be reflected by competency issues, but that decision is best made by the jury, which has all the case facts before it. Much of the effort to exempt the "mentally retarded" from execution can best be described as another effort to reduce the application of a proper sentencing option by those who oppose executions under all circumstances.

3. In establishing a below 70 IQ number as the threshold for withholding a death sentence option, several important issues are often neglected: a) the previously discussed issue of both the 10 point variable and the performance IQ issues, as well as b) when the IQ test was taken. If the test was taken after an arrest, then there is a strong likelihood that the arrested party would do everything possible to score as low as possible, as a self preservation issue. This would negate the reliability of the test. And as you can never be sure about that issue, under those circumstances, then other means will have to be used to establish competency and c) IQ tests results, with the same individual, can vary greatly over time, well outside any 10 point variable. This directly goes to those states which have standards that say the test must have been administered prior to age 18. Both education and experience can increase IQs over time. Therefore,

that prior to age 18 rule may allow a competent murderer to escape proper punishment, only because of an arbitrary and capricious standard, which had no relevance at the time of the murder. And, again, the distinction between general and performance IQ comes into play, as well as all the other variables and limitations.

That is why the current system, as it now exists, is the best. Determine competency pre-trial. Relive those issues again, at trial and on appeal. Establish if the defendant knew right from wrong, if the defendants can constructively participate in their own defense and establish if they understand the nature of their punishment. And review those issues, again, on appeal.

That appears to be the most responsible and honest method of reviewing these cases and issues. Any other method is more arbitrary and capricious. To date, there is nothing to indicate that a better system has been presented. If you review those state statutes which ban the death penalty for the "mentally retarded," you will find that virtually all of them have some problems which make their death penalty statutes more arbitrary and capricious and which do not reflect a full appreciation of the issues. In effect, what many of those states have done is to pass laws which will allow fully competent murderers to escape the most appropriate punishment consideration. Remember, these statutes are specifically directed against the death sentence, not lesser sentences.

5

The Death Penalty Is Biased in Favor of Women

Cathy Young

Cathy Young is the author of Ceasefire! Why Women and Men Must Join Forces to Achieve True Equality.

Gender bias is apparent in the application of the death penalty. Women are less likely to be executed than men are for committing similar kinds of murders, and women are more likely than men to have their death sentences commuted. This unequal administration of capital punishment is largely due to a paternal sexism that manifests itself in an overprotectiveness toward women. Female murderers, for example, garner more sympathy because they tend to be perceived as victims of abuse or despair and not as calculating killers. Making such excuses for female violence undermines the goals of feminism because it denies women's moral accountability.

O n a Tuesday night in Varner, Ark., 28-year-old Christina Marie Riggs was executed for the 1997 murders of her two small children. She was given a lethal injection of potassium chloride, the drug she had originally planned to use to kill her children. (She suffocated them after a botched attempt of the drugging plan.)

Riggs, a former nurse, was put to death despite pleas for her life from anti-death-penalty groups including Amnesty International and the American Civil Liberties Union. In fact, there was little difference between the execution of Riggs and the other executions carried out in the United States in the year 2000 except that Riggs, who said she wanted to die to be with her "babies," had refused to appeal her sentence or to seek clemency from Arkansas Gov. Mike Huckabee.

And yet her death was much bigger news.

Garden-variety sexism

The cause for intense public soul-searching and beating of breasts was not the nature of Riggs' crime or her wish to die. It was her gender. It was, for all intents and purposes, a demonstration of garden-variety sexism. And this isn't the first time our hypocrisy has been blatantly displayed.

Riggs was the first woman to be executed in Arkansas in 150 years, and only the fifth executed in the nation since the U.S. Supreme Court lifted the ban on capital punishment in 1976. Obviously, the very rarity of women's executions makes them newsworthy. But this is only the statistical manifestation of the stubborn gender discrimination that taints our attitude about capital punishment in this country.

Whether one sees the death penalty as justice or barbarism (and, for the record, I have no moral objection to imposing it for premeditated murder, though the risk of the state taking an innocent life is troubling enough to warrant opposition to the practice), surely the perpetrator's gender should be irrelevant.

But that is not the way it works in the real world. We are consistently more likely to seek mitigating circumstances for women's heinous deeds, to see female criminals as disturbed or victimized rather than evil. The thought of a woman in the death chamber makes people cringe—even those who have no problem with sending a man to his death for his crimes.

It appears that chivalry still lives when a woman must die.

In 1998, there were many more headlines and much more debate as Karla Faye Tucker awaited execution in Texas for a brutal double murder. Tucker had become a born-again Christian and her clemency petition was backed by such unusual suspects as Christian Coalition leader Pat Robertson, Moral Majority founder Jerry Falwell and right-wing hero Oliver North—all generally pro-capital punishment.

While most of Tucker's champions insisted that redemption and not womanhood was the issue, none had intervened on behalf of male murderers who had experienced similar death-row conversions. And there was ample evidence to suggest that the support for "this sweet woman of God," as Robertson put it, was not entirely gender-neutral.

On CNN's *Crossfire*, when asked if the crusade to save Tucker was an instance of "misplaced chivalry," North gallantly replied, "I don't think chivalry can ever be misplaced"—though he went on to insist that "gender is not a factor." Meanwhile, on the left, the chivalrous Geraldo Rivera dispensed with any pretense of neutrality and issued a bizarre plea to Texas Gov. George W. Bush on his CNBC show: "Please, don't let this happen. This is—it's very unseemly. Texas, manhood, macho swagger . . . What are ya, going to kill a lady? Oh, jeez. Why?"

The lady in question, by the way, had used a pickax to dispatch two sleeping people (one of whom had made her angry by parking his motorbike in her living room) and later bragged that she experienced an orgasm with every swing.

A double standard

Some criminal justice experts, such as Victor Streib, dean of the law college at Ohio Northern University, argue that the double standard favoring women kicks in long before the final death watch, and that women offenders are "screened out at all levels of the system." Women commit about 10 percent of all murders in the U.S., yet receive only about 2 percent of the death sentences and account for about 1 percent of death-row inmates, since their sentences are more often commuted or reversed.

True, numbers don't tell the whole story. Male killers are more likely to have committed the kinds of crimes that make them eligible for a death sentence, from cop-killing to murder during the commission of another crime such as robbery. When women kill, their victims are more likely to be family members, including their own children—which, rightly or not, tends to be treated as a lesser crime.

Women commit about 10 percent of all murders in the U.S., yet receive only about 2 percent of the death sentences.

Still, it is worth noting that while women commit nearly 30 percent of spousal murders (excluding homicides ruled to be in self-defense), they account for only 15 percent of prisoners sentenced to death for killing a spouse.

And the disparity between the treatment of male and female defendants can be stunning when you look beyond the numbers. In 1995, Texas executed Jesse Dewayne Jacobs for a murder that, by the prosecutors' admission, was committed by his sister Bobbie Jean Hogan. It was Hogan who had gotten her brother to help her abduct Etta Ann Urdiales—her boyfriend's ex-wife who was making vexatious demands for child support—and who had actually pulled the trigger.

When Hogan went on trial, separately from her brother and co-conspirator, her lawyers managed to persuade the jury that the gun went off accidentally and obtained a verdict of involuntary manslaughter. She received a 10-year prison sentence.

Maybe we don't know for certain that gender bias played a role in these different outcomes. Two male accomplices in a crime can receive strikingly disparate sentences, since much depends on the personalities of the jurors and the quality of the defense. But it's hardly a stretch to conclude that gender matters. Jurors may not intentionally go easy on women, but they may be far more inclined to believe that a gun was not fired on purpose if it was in a woman's hands. How many times have we seen that one in the movies?

And then there is the perennial persuader in consideration of a woman's fate before the law: sympathy. When Susan Smith sent her two little sons into the muddy waters of a lake strapped into their car seats, apparently because they were an obstacle to her love life, and made up a story about a black carjacker, she was initially denounced as a cold-blooded monster.

Yet even *her* image underwent a gradual shift, with revelations that she had been molested by her stepfather as a teen (even though, somewhat less sympathetically, she had continued carrying on an affair with him as an adult and married woman) and suggestions that her no-good husband was really to blame for her anguish (even though there was little reason to believe that he was any more responsible for the breakdown of the marriage than she was). "This is not a case about evil," Smith's attorney, Judy Clarke, told the jury that gave her life in prison. "It is about despair and sadness."

Smith may have cut a pitiable figure. So, apparently, did Guinevere Garcia, who fatally shot her husband for his insurance money 14 years after she had suffocated her 11-month-old daughter—and whose death sentence was commuted to life in prison by Illinois Gov. Jim Edgar in 1996.

Garcia had been sexually abused as a child and was an alcoholic prostitute by the age of 15. But the same was true of Jesse Timmendequas, the sex offender awaiting execution in New Jersey for strangling five-year-old Megan Kanka, the child who gave her name to "Megan's law." According to trial evidence, Timmendequas had been brutally beaten and sodomized by his father.

In fact, nearly half of male death-row inmates claim to have been physically abused in their childhood, while more than 1 in 4 say that they were sexually molested. Of course, some of these claims of victimization may be self-serving, but then again, not every woman's abuse excuse is the gospel truth.

Of course, not everyone champions gender neutrality when it comes to crime and punishment. Some find the fair sex to be justified in getting unfair treatment. "Women and men do occupy separate places in the collective psyche of society," Jonathan Last wrote in the conservative *Weekly Standard* shortly after Tucker's execution. "Because society has a low tolerance for seeing them harmed, women—even criminals—have traditionally been treated differently by the justice system. Differently, but still, at least possibly, with justice. The loss of that difference is part of what makes [the] destruction of Karla Faye Tucker so disturbing."

This sort of paternalism—which, as Last explicitly stated, also provides the justification for keeping women out of combat forces—seems precisely the sort of sugar-and-spice rationalization that feminists ought to oppose. Yet they have remained largely silent on the subject, for several reasons. One is that when feminism becomes a movement for the advantage of women (rather than for equal treatment), complaining about favoritism toward women doesn't make a lot of sense.

> *While women commit nearly 30 percent of spousal murders, . . . they account for only 15 percent of prisoners sentenced to death for killing a spouse.*

Many also find it hard to admit the basic fact that in Western societies in the modern era, patriarchal norms have revolved less around the subjugation of women through violence—one of the feminists' favorite themes—than around less protectiveness toward women.

Far from denouncing double standards, many feminists have contributed to the excuse-making. When Betty Lou Beets, 62, was facing execution in Texas in February for the murder of her fifth husband, Jimmy Don Beets, battered women's advocates rallied to her defense, portraying her as a victim of years of domestic abuse. Beets had been convicted of shooting and wounding her second husband, Bill Lane, and had been charged but never tried in the 1981 death of husband No. 4, Doyle Barker. Beets had never claimed to have been battered during her trial, and had tried to blame the slaying on her two children.

The victim sweepstakes

Even when the death penalty is not at issue and even when there are no allegations of physical abuse, murderous women can still qualify for life-saving prizes in the victim sweepstakes.

Some years ago, Betty Broderick, the California housewife who killed her wealthy ex-husband and his young new wife—and claimed that the divorce and the alimony payments of $16,000 a month amounted to "white-collar domestic violence"—became the subject of sympathetic profiles in *Ladies' Home Journal* and *Mirabella*.

An essay in a feminist anthology on women and violence, *No Angels* (1996), lamented that support for battered women who fight back had not extended to "fighting back against an emotionally abusive husband" and denounced a TV movie portraying Broderick in a negative light as "misogynist."

Contrary to all the evidence, feminists also have asserted that it's women who are treated with extra harshness by the system. In her 1996 book *Still Unequal: The Shameful Truth About Women and Justice in America* Lorraine Dusky asserts that women receive "more severe sentences" for stereotypically male crimes, though she cites no evidence to support this. But according to a 1989 Bureau of Justice Statistics study, male violent offenders were more than twice as likely as women charged with similar crimes to be incarcerated for more than a year.

Other research has found that, even when factors such as severity of the offense and prior criminal record are taken into account, women are more likely to have charges dismissed or to receive a light sentence.

Advocates for battered women also have claimed that a woman who kills her mate is sentenced to an average of 15 to 20 years in prison, while a man gets two to six years. This appalling factoid seems to be pure fiction. A Justice Department study of domestic homicides paints a very different picture: Husbands who killed their wives received an average of 16.5 years in prison; wives who killed husbands got six years. While some of the disparity was due to the fact that more women had been "provoked"—assaulted or threatened—before the slaying, the study noted that "the average prison sentence for unprovoked wife defendants was seven years, or 10 years shorter than the average 17 years for the unprovoked husband defendants."

If one truly believes in the full equality of the sexes, it's not difficult to see that protectiveness toward women, whether motivated by chivalry or feminism, keeps us from achieving a legitimate goal. As Patricia Pearson argues in her 1997 book *When She Was Bad: Violent Women and the Myth of Innocence,* making excuses for women's violence ultimately strips them of moral agency and accountability. What does it say about women's ability to function in society, to be workers and leaders, if they are seen as more vulnerable to pressure and more easily forgiven for failing to cope with their emotional problems?

If women are to be treated as adults, we cannot recoil from the execution of a woman the way we do from the execution of a juvenile. The debate about capital punishment should focus on humanity, not womanhood. To demand equality—yet ask for a special right to clemency—just won't do.

6

A Moratorium on Executions Is Justified

George H. Ryan

George H. Ryan is the Republican governor of Illinois.

Investigations of death-penalty cases in Illinois have revealed a pattern of discrimination, legal and judicial flaws, and wrongful convictions. Most startling was the revelation in the year 2000 that thirteen of the state's death-row inmates had been declared innocent of the crimes they were originally convicted for—one more than the twelve who had already been executed since the reinstatement of the death penalty in Illinois. The gubernatorial moratorium on executions that was declared on January 31, 2000, was an ethical decision. Capital punishment should be suspended until the legal system can ensure that no innocents are put to death.

Editor's note: In January 2003, George H. Ryan granted clemency to all of Illinois' death-row inmates, commuting most of the state's death sentences to sentences of life without parole.

A s a member of the Illinois General Assembly, I vividly remember voting for the death penalty. During the debate, an opponent of the death penalty asked whether any of us who supported it would be willing to "throw the switch." It was a sobering question, and I wish now that I could swallow the words of unqualified support for the death penalty that I offered.

The fact is now as governor, I do "throw the switch." That's the toughest part of being governor.

I don't know that courage is the best word to describe what I did in the year 2000 in declaring a moratorium on the death penalty. I just call it doing the right thing. All I did was to respond to the indisputable facts—that the administration of the death penalty in Illinois was not fair, and our record was shameful.

I've been in elective office for more than 30 years. During that time,

George H. Ryan, "Illinois Needed Moratorium on Death Penalty," *State Government News*, vol. 44, May 2001, p. 10. Copyright © 2001 by the Council of State Governments. Reproduced by permission.

as a county board member, legislator and executive officeholder, I was a staunch supporter of the death penalty. Like many other elected officials, I have believed there are crimes that are so heinous that the death sentence is the only proper, societal response for the criminals convicted of those crimes in a court of law.

Since those days as a legislator, a lot has happened to shake my faith in the death-penalty system. I know a lot more about the administration of the death penalty in Illinois—and the more I learn, the more troubled I've become.

An eye-opening investigation

In November 1999, the *Chicago Tribune* conducted an in-depth investigation of the death-penalty cases in Illinois that was startling. Half of the nearly 300 capital cases in the state had been reversed for a new trial or sentencing hearing. Thirty-three of the death-row inmates had been represented at trial by an attorney who had later been disbarred or at some point suspended from practicing law. Thirty-five African-Americans on death row had been convicted or condemned by an all-white jury. In fact, two out of three of our 160 Illinois death-row inmates are African-American. Prosecutors used jailhouse informants to convict or condemn 46 death-row inmates.

In January of 2000, the 13th inmate on death-row was found wrongfully convicted of the murder for which he had been sentenced to die. At that point, I was looking at our shameful scorecard. We had 13 people exonerated of their crimes for which they had been sentenced to die—more than the 12 we had convicted and executed since the death penalty had been reinstated. Thirteen people who lived the ultimate nightmare—sitting on death-row, waiting to be killed by the state for crimes they did not commit.

Up until then, with each remarkable, complex and sometimes confusing development, I had resisted calls by some to declare a moratorium on executions. But then I had to ask myself: How could I go forward with so many unanswered questions? It was clear to me that when it came to the death penalty in Illinois, there was no justice in the justice system.

On Jan. 31, 2000, I told the citizens of Illinois that I was imposing a moratorium on executions because of grave concerns about our state's record of convicting innocent people and putting them on death row. I said that a public dialogue must begin on the question of the fairness of the application of the death penalty. That, surely, has taken place since I announced my decision.

In March of 2000 I empaneled a commission of 14 concerned, smart and honorable people. My instructions to the committee were simple: Until I can be sure that everyone sentenced to death in Illinois is truly guilty, and until I can be sure with moral certainty that no innocent person is facing a lethal injection, no one will meet that fate.

I am comfortable knowing that I did the right thing.

7

Wrongful Executions Are Not Likely to Occur

Eugene H. Methvin

Eugene H. Methvin is a Reader's Digest *contributing editor based in Washington, D.C.*

Fears about the possibility of executing innocent inmates are unfounded. No one has proven that any wrongful executions have occurred. Furthermore, technological advances such as DNA testing now enable investigators to present proof that exonerates the wrongly convicted; DNA evidence also allows law enforcement officials to close in on actual criminals more quickly. The numerous appeals that are typically granted to convicts also make it improbable that innocent people could be executed.

If there's been a change in the death-penalty winds, it's because capital-punishment opponents have been fanning a national panic over the chance that we might be putting innocent people to death. The truth is, we've never been better positioned to ascertain guilt or innocence.

In April 2000, Illinois Gov. George Ryan declared a moratorium on executions in his state. A Republican who favors capital punishment, Mr. Ryan nonetheless said Illinois had a "shameful record" of condemning innocent people to die. He based his decision in part on the case of Steve Manning, a former Chicago cop who in January 2000, became the 13th man exonerated from Illinois's death row since 1976. [Editor's note: In January 2003, Ryan commuted Illinois' death sentences to life sentences without parole.]

Mr. Ryan isn't the only Republican calling for a rethinking of the death penalty. In April 2000, televangelist Pat Robertson joined the American Civil Liberties Union [ACLU] in asking for a nationwide moratorium on executions. Widespread coverage has followed a new book, *Actual Innocence: Five Days to Execution and Other Dispatches From the Wrongly Convicted*, written by two lawyers and a journalist who claim DNA is proving appalling miscarriages of justice. And in May 2000, New York Gov. George Pataki proposed a state DNA review committee to examine all convictions overturned because of new genetic evidence.

Mistakes are rare

Some of the scrutiny is justified. Illinois has set a national record over the past decade for convicting cops and judges in federal corruption probes, and the state has had some close calls—one death-row prisoner came within two days of execution before he was exonerated. And certainly no one can say unequivocally that no innocent person in the U.S. has been wrongly executed, or that it can't happen.

But so far no one has demonstrated that it has. Quite the opposite. With the average time consumed by appeals between sentencing and execution now at about 10 years, and with the arrival of DNA testing in the 1990s, the likelihood of wrongful executions is less than ever.

Opponents of capital punishment have pointed to the work of two abolitionist scholars, Hugo Bedau and Michael Radelet, who claimed they found 23 instances of convicts executed between 1900 and 1986 who were later proved innocent. But only one of these executions occurred after 1976, when the Supreme Court radically revamped death-penalty procedures. Moreover, the scholars appear to have based their conclusions on defendants' briefs, newspaper stories, defense-attorney claims or lapses in prosecutor conduct or trial procedure.

Stephen Markman and Paul Cassell, two Justice Department lawyers during the Reagan administration, reviewed 13 of the 23 cases—every one since 1950, the date after which they could get original court records. Based on these actual transcripts, they demonstrated that the alleged executed innocents were "guilty as sin," and that, at least since 1950, there was no documented case of innocent individuals executed. In all 13 cases, they noted, the trial records contained eyewitness testimony, confessions, or circumstantial and physical evidence demonstrating guilt. If anything, said Mr. Markman, the Bedau-Radelet study "speaks eloquently about the extraordinary rarity of error in capital punishment."

A Virginia case

Virginia's 1992 execution of Roger Keith Coleman illustrates the point. An articulate liar and manipulator, Coleman had already served a 20-month prison term for attempted rape. Yet after an unspeakable rape-murder, he mobilized America's vocal abolitionist minority and conned the media into portraying him as the innocent victim of backwoods justice.

On March 10, 1981, Coleman went to the home of his sister-in-law, whose husband was at work, cut her throat and raped her. Blood stains on his pants, semen matching Coleman's rare blood type, and witnesses' testimony—not to mention his own lies about his movements that night—persuaded a jury to convict him.

In 1990 Kitty Behan, a former ACLU lawyer with the high-powered Washington law firm of Arnold & Porter, mounted a legal and media blitz to save him. Ms. Behan got a court order requiring a newly developed DNA test on the semen. But the highly respected expert she chose found the test pointed unmistakably to Coleman. She then hired another "expert" to dispute these findings. She issued press releases accusing another man of the murder. The man sued for libel, and Ms. Behan's law firm reportedly paid an out-of-court settlement.

Still, Ms. Behan's media blitz had an effect. Both *Newsweek* and *Time* ran stories portraying Coleman as an innocent victim. Neither magazine mentioned the damning DNA evidence. When U.S. District Judge Glen Williams reviewed the evidence, he declared: "This court finds the case against Coleman as strong or stronger than the evidence adduced at trial." Eleven years after he murdered his sister-in-law, Coleman was executed. But he left millions fearing an innocent man had been murdered by the justice system.

Procedural difficulties

Many death-row convictions are overturned not on questions of guilt but on procedural grounds, in a judicial war against the death penalty. The Georgia Supreme Court in March 2000 overturned the death sentence of a killer who nearly decapitated a former girlfriend. The court found the prosecutor had wrongly urged jurors to follow the biblical mandate: "All they who take up the sword shall die by the sword." Departing from prior decisions approving biblical arguments, Justice Norman Fletcher decreed: "Biblical references . . . improperly appeal to the religious beliefs of jurors."

Multiple appeals . . . make executing the innocent more unlikely than ever.

Other judges have voided death sentences because jurors weren't told the killer would otherwise get life without parole. Prosecutors, however, are forbidden to argue that killers might escape, which they do, even from high-security facilities.

Multiple appeals not only make executing the innocent more unlikely than ever, they make it hard to execute the clearly guilty. Illinois executed John Wayne Gacy in 1994 for murdering 33 young men. He had confessed, and his guilt was never in the slightest doubt. Yet his lawyers consumed 14 years with legal delays. "He had 523 separate appeals," fumes House Judiciary Chairman Henry Hyde (R., Ill.). "And none were based on a claim of innocence."

Things haven't changed much since then. On the first anniversary of the Oklahoma City bombing, Congress passed the Antiterrorism and Effective Death Penalty Act. For the first time in 128 years, legislators used their constitutional authority to strip the Supreme Court and lower federal judges of jurisdiction to hear appeals for a certain class of case.

Even under this change, a state convict can still have 10 appeals (in some cases 12), before the new law affects him. He can go through five or six state and federal courts on direct appeal, then go through them again with habeas corpus petitions. But for a second federal habeas corpus review, Congress decreed, convicts must get permission from a three-judge federal appeals panel. If he is turned down, the Supreme Court can grant only one further review, and only in rare circumstances.

As for DNA, that is doing much more than just helping re-evaluate convictions. At least 64 U.S. criminal convictions have been set aside as a result of DNA testing, according to the Innocence Project of the Cardozo

Law School at Yeshiva University. But DNA testing also allows investigators to eliminate many suspects early on, and concentrate on pursuing the real perpetrators.

Even Hugo Bedau, a professor at Tufts University and a leading abolitionist, has admitted that it is "false sentimentality to argue that the death penalty ought to be abolished because of the abstract possibility that an innocent person might be executed when the record fails to disclose that such cases occur." That drunk drivers kill thousands of innocents, that airplanes fall, that pedestrians get smashed by cars, does not prevent us from drinking, flying or crossing the street. But the possibility that an innocent person may be executed is supposed to make us give up capital punishment because "death is irrevocable."

Compelled to administer justice in an imperfect world, we should not allow a utopian yearning for perfect certainty to render us moral eunuchs. As George Washington wrote a friend on the eve of the Constitutional Convention, "Perfection falls not to the lot of mortal man. We must take men as we find them."

8

The Possibility of Wrongful Executions Justifies Abolishing the Death Penalty

Carl M. Cannon

Carl M. Cannon is the White House correspondent for National Journal *and president of the White House Correspondents Association.*

Execution is a seemingly moral and just punishment for those who commit felony murder. However, in recent years, several death-row prisoners have escaped execution after postconviction DNA evidence proved that they were innocent. Such cases reveal the unreliability of the judicial branch of government and call into question the legitimacy of capital punishment as it is administered in the United States. Since it has been proven that a certain percentage of condemned inmates are actually innocent, the death penalty should be abolished.

At a dinner party in Georgetown during the Reagan years, I was seated next to a liberal journalist I didn't know too well—Sidney Blumenthal, then with *The New Republic*. No matter what has happened since, he was erudite and charming that night as we discussed the Washington scene. But my mind was largely elsewhere, for that week I had begun work on a story about a man convicted of murder who was possibly innocent. I was preoccupied, not with anything the administration might have been doing, but with the issue of capital punishment.

At some point, I asked my dinner companion his view of the death penalty.

"Oh, we're against it," he replied.

I recall being amused by that pronoun, "we"—Whom did he mean? The Democratic party? The elites?—but eventually I decided he meant the magazine he worked for. I asked him why.

"The moral issue," he said.

I remember also that this remark antagonized me. I do not support capital punishment either, but this was so inadequate an answer that I

Carl M. Cannon, "The Problem with the Chair—A Conservative Case Against Capital Punishment," *National Review*, vol. 52, June 19, 2000. Copyright © 2000 by National Review, Inc. Reproduced by permission.

found myself arguing the other side of the question. I did so by invoking the specter of Steven Timothy Judy.

The case of Steven Judy

On April 28, 1979, Judy was cruising down the highway when he came across 23-year-old Terry Lee Chasteen, who was stranded with her kids by the side of the road in her disabled vehicle. Pretending to be a Good Samaritan, Steven Judy further disabled Chasteen's car by disconnecting the ignition wires, then drove her and her three children—Misty Ann, 5, Steve, 4, and Mark, 2—to a secluded location. He raped and strangled Chasteen and drowned the children, one by one, in a nearby creek.

Judy was quickly arrested and convicted of capital murder. At trial, he assured the jurors that if they didn't vote for the death penalty he'd kill again someday. "And it may be one of you next," he warned. "Or your family."

The jury obliged, and on March 9, 1981, the state of Indiana put Steven Judy to death in an electric chair nicknamed "Old Betsy." The "moral" aspect of allowing Judy to live eluded the grasp of not just me, but a majority of Americans. Except to the most ideological of criminal-justice liberals—and perhaps to Judy's fellow inmates at his Michigan City prison—his execution seemed a blow in behalf of civilization.

But if Judy's crimes were hideous even by the grisly standards of Death Row, what makes his case notable almost 20 years later is that his execution—or rather, the lack of an outcry at his execution—was a signal that a momentous change was taking place in America. Until that night, there had been only three executions in the United States since the confusing 5-4 Supreme Court decision in 1976 invalidating all existing state death-penalty laws. But the states inclined to use this remedy had hurriedly rewritten their statutes to conform with the Court's requirements, and just five years later here was Steven Judy saying to the guards as he was strapped into Old Betsy, "I don't hold no grudges. This is my doing. . . ."

It was not generally apparent then that a flood of executions was about to begin. Judy's case seemed unproblematic in that he had not appealed his sentence. In so refusing, he had followed in the footsteps of Gary Mark Gilmore, executed by firing squad in Utah in 1977, and Jesse Bishop, who went to Nevada's gas chamber in 1979. John Spenkelink, electrocuted in Florida in 1979 after spurning a plea bargain that would have earned him a measly 20 years in prison—he argued self-defense—was the only one of the four to go to his death unwillingly. But it was the business-as-usual aspect of the Judy case that served as a portent.

Thanks to the added tool of DNA evidence, the true horror of the death penalty has made itself plain.

The night he was executed, liberal activists descended on Michigan City in a familiar ritual: the candlelight vigil. A crowd of some 200 of them braved the wind and rain to be there, but they were not alone. Earlier, at a "Protect the Innocent" rally in a downtown park, Mark Chasteen, the slain woman's ex-husband, assured a pro-death penalty crowd that he'd "throw the switch" himself. As the hour approached, motorists passing the prison would slow down, honk their horns, and yell, "Burn, Judy!"

On that March night, the United States was heading briskly down a road it had not taken since the rough days of the Great Depression. Not much longer would executions be international news events. In a handful of states, most prominently Texas, they would actually become routine. In fact, within two years, crowds of several hundred Texans would be rallying outside the Huntsville prison on execution nights to celebrate. Battered by a violent-crime rate that threatened the very freedoms we are promised in our founding documents, and angered by repeated accounts of vicious predators who were paroled only to kill again, Americans were calling for a remedy prescribed long ago: "An eye for an eye!" demonstrators would chant.

Should [the government] be in the business of executing people convicted of murder knowing to a certainty that some of them are innocent[?]

And who can argue with this ancient wisdom? Well, I will. What if the issue is not an eye for an eye, but an eye for a finger? Or removing the eye of someone you thought put out your eye, but, in fact, only looks like the guy who did? This is not an academic question, and it never has been. And now, thanks to several high-profile cases in which condemned men were exonerated, and thanks to the added tool of DNA evidence, the true horror of the death penalty has made itself plain. The right question to ask is not whether capital punishment is an appropriate—or a moral—response to murders. It is whether the government should be in the business of executing people convicted of murder knowing to a certainty that some of them are innocent.

An old fight

Chicago, where Sid Blumenthal hails from, has long occupied center stage in the timeless debate over capital punishment. Seventy-five years ago, the liberal lawyer and activist Clarence Darrow convened weekly meetings in his Chicago home to discuss the social issues of the day. Paul Cline, my grandmother's husband, attended some of those meetings. I asked him once which discussions he remembered best. His answer: Those in which the great defense lawyer inveighed against capital punishment. Then, as now, the Left considered this remedy barbaric and capricious. It was, they said, applied too easily to the poor and the politically unpopular, especially to blacks, to whom the gallows were akin to lynching. Innocence was raised as an issue by liberals, but then, as now, it was not their primary objection.

Darrow was faced with a subtle dilemma, therefore, when he was retained as defense counsel in the Roaring Twenties' most sensational murder case, the Leopold and Loeb trial. These defendants were not poor or black or immigrants or involved in unpopular political causes. They were, in fact, white, rich, well educated, and not politically active—and their lawyer agreed that they were guilty as hell. In his impassioned closing argument, Darrow actually alluded to the internal conflict this presented for him, even as he labored to spare Nathan Leopold and Richard Loeb the noose.

Juries make mistakes all the time. . . . [Sometimes] they convict innocent people.

"This case may not be as important as I think it is, and I am sure I do not need to tell this court, or to tell my friends, that I would fight just as hard for the poor as for the rich," said Darrow during his historic twelve-hour summation. "If I should succeed in saving these boys' lives and do nothing for the progress of the law, I should feel sad, indeed."

Darrow did save the "boys'" lives—at least one of them, anyway (Loeb was stabbed to death in the Joliet prison in 1936)—and he probably did much for the progress of the law as he saw it, too. His closing was taught in law schools for generations afterward, and it is still venerated by legal scholars who oppose capital punishment. "It left the presiding judge in tears," notes Douglas O. Linder of the University of Missouri, Kansas City. "People still think of his summation in the Leopold-Loeb case as one of the most eloquent attacks on the death penalty ever made."

But a perusal of Darrow's argument today is not likely to reduce many conservatives to tears, or even sympathy. Although Darrow based much of his argument for mercy on the fact that neither defendant had yet reached his 20th birthday, the lawyer was also an avowed determinist who seemed to hold the defendants nearly blameless for their vicious crime. He also spent much of his time arguing that history was on a long, inexorable march away from capital punishment and that future generations would consider hanging as barbaric as crucifixion and burning at the stake. A modern conservative reading the trial transcript is more likely to identify with state's attorney Robert Crowe, a gifted Yale Law School graduate who was at the time a rising star in Illinois Republican politics.

In his closing argument, Crowe sarcastically characterized Darrow as "the distinguished gentleman whose profession it is to protect murder in Cook County and whose health thieves inquire about before they go and commit a crime." The term "junk science" was not yet in vogue, but the prosecutor accused a defense psychiatrist of "prostituting his profession" and mocked Darrow's argument that the defendants weren't ultimately to blame for their actions: "My God, if one of them had a harelip I suppose Darrow would want me to apologize for having them indicted."

A governor doubts

And so it went for three-quarters of a century, during which the arguments for and against capital punishment barely changed at all—until the year 2000, that is. The governor of Illinois—a conservative, Republican governor named George Ryan—read about one too many cases of Death Row inmates' being freed in his state because of new evidence that showed they were innocent of the crime. "Until I can be sure that everyone sentenced to death in Illinois is truly guilty; until I can be sure, with moral certainty, that no innocent man or woman is facing a lethal injection, no one will meet that fate," Ryan said. "I cannot support a system which, in its administration, has proven so fraught with error and has come so close to the ultimate nightmare, the state's taking of innocent life."

As many now know, 13 inmates condemned to death by the state of Illinois have been cleared of capital-murder charges in the [more than] 23 years since capital punishment was reinstated. During this time, the state has executed a dozen inmates convicted of murder, a ratio of governmental failure so alarming that it struck the man ultimately responsible for carrying out the death penalty in a very personal way. "There's going to be a lot of folks who are firm believers in the death penalty who may not agree with what I'm doing here today," Ryan explained. "But I am the fellow who has to make the ultimate decision whether someone is injected with a poison that's going to take their life . . ." [Editor's note: In 2003, Ryan commuted Illinois' death sentences into life sentences without parole.]

The governor also cited a *Chicago Tribune* investigative series that examined each of the state's nearly 300 capital cases and found that these trials were routinely riddled with bias and error, including incompetent legal work by the defense lawyers, and that prosecutors relied on dubious jailhouse informants in about 50 of the cases. Two of the Illinois exonerations were brought about by Northwestern University professor Lawrence Marshall, who took on the cases without a fee. In one case, that of Rolando Cruz, Marshall's work resulted in 1) the freeing of an innocent man after twelve years on Death Row for the murder and rape of a ten-year-old girl, 2) criminal charges against the authorities who prosecuted Cruz, and 3) the identification of the actual killer.

How many innocent people were executed in the years before DNA tests became available?

The most famous reversals in Illinois came about because journalism students at Northwestern kept unearthing evidence that exonerated various convicts on Death Row. For example, four black men from Detroit had been convicted of abducting a white couple, raping the woman and killing both her and the man. Two of the four, Dennis Williams and Verneal Jimerson, were sentenced to death. Students under the direction of journalism professor David Protess investigated the case and discovered that the prosecution's star witness had an IQ of less than 75 and that prosecutors had fed her details of the crime and coached her into testifying about them.

Public pressure because of these revelations forced the district attorney's office to allow DNA tests—which promptly eliminated as suspects all four of the men convicted of the crime. The students, going through the records of the case, found something even more stunning in the state's files: the names of four other suspects who'd been identified to authorities, but never even questioned by the police. The students interviewed three of them (the fourth, the ringleader, had since died), and, incredibly, all three eventually confessed. They are now serving life sentences.

Then, in 1999, Prof. Protess and five of his students, working with a private detective, wormed a confession out of a drug dealer for a 1982 double murder for which another man, Anthony Porter, had been convicted. Not just convicted, but sentenced to death. In September 1998, in fact, Porter had been two days away from execution when a state appeals court issued a stay to consider whether it was constitutional to execute someone with Porter's IQ (estimated at 51). It turns out his IQ is a bit higher than that, but the point is that the delay in the execution gave the Northwestern team time to dig through the records and finger the man who subsequently confessed to the crime.

"I know that we have, on occasions in the past, executed those people who are in fact innocent," [Gerald] Kogan said at a Capitol Hill press conference.

"The judicial system commits errors," commented Prof. Protess, in a classic understatement, "because it's run by people."

This simple observation shouldn't come as a bolt from the blue—least of all to conservatives. It just shouldn't be a surprise that civil servants take shortcuts on the job, that juries drawn from the citizenry that gives former president Bill Clinton a 60 percent approval rating [after he was accused of lying after having sex with White House aide Monica Lewinsky] get swept up in the passions of the day, that political hacks appointed to the bench ratify those mistakes, and that bloated state-run bureaucracies are loath to correct them. "Criminal-justice system" is a high falutin phrase, but the courts are just a branch of government, and one that by design has less accountability than the other two.

In other words, if ideology and experience lead one to the conclusion that government is by nature inefficient and inept, then why should it be astonishing that the actions of one branch of government—the judicial branch—are so routinely wrong?

One reporter's experience

I will return to this point, but before I do, I want to explain why I am absolutely certain that this is a universal problem, that there is nothing aberrant about the Illinois courts. Before I was 30 years old, I covered four cases in which defendants were charged with capital murder, but were, in fact, completely innocent. (In a fifth case, a man from Petersburg, Virginia— George Roberts—was convicted of killing his wife, served seven years, and after being paroled, convinced the local cops that he'd been framed.)

In the first of these cases, police in Columbus, Georgia, arrested a black man named Jerome Livas and charged him with strangling and raping two elderly white women. No physical evidence linked Livas to the crimes, he did not fit the psychological profile produced by the FBI, and he was borderline mentally retarded (the crimes had been meticulously planned and carried out). When the killings continued with the identical method of operation while Livas was locked up in jail, the cops blithely offered the cockamamie theory that a copycat killer must be on the loose. Livas, they said, had confessed and—this is a phrase that often comes up in these cases—possessed details "only the killer would know."

I covered the police beat in that town for the local paper, and a friendly cop called me at home one night to tell me that all those supposedly confidential details had, in fact, been fed to Livas by the detectives themselves, and that Livas was so unintelligent and so eager to please that he'd just parroted them back to the investigators. "This guy would admit to anything," said the cop. Subsequently I tested that theory in a session the *Washington Post* dubbed "a sensational jailhouse interview." It was sensational, all right, but sad. I succeeded in getting Livas to sign a confession for killing Presidents John F. Kennedy and William McKinley and for kidnapping the Lindbergh baby. Red-faced authorities dropped the charges against Livas, and years later, long after I'd left Columbus, they got the right man—presumably—and he was executed. But it's pretty clear to me what would have happened to Jerome Livas if the real murderer had stopped killing when Livas was arrested.

> *In the face of the awful truth presented to us by DNA testing, what name shall we call the state-sanctioned killing of an innocent man?*

I'm a Californian, so there was in those years a temptation to think that such miscarriages happen only in the Deep South or in jerkwater towns—but this proved not to be true. They can happen anywhere, in towns big and small, and they do. In my next job, at the *San Diego Union*, I was working the police beat when the Los Angeles Police Department (LAPD) publicly fingered a Massachusetts convict named George Francis Shamshak as a suspect in the so-called Hillside Stranglings. Daryl Gates, then the head of the Hillside Strangler Task Force, later to be famous (or infamous) as chief of the LAPD, even used that ubiquitous phrase "knowledge only the killer would have" to explain why they were sure they had the right guy. Except that Shamshak was in prison in Massachusetts when some of the killings took place, a fact I pointed out to Gates myself at an entertaining news conference. The details only the killer would know? Turns out that he'd read them in *Newsweek*.

In the early 1980s, a gifted investigative journalist named Jon Standefer and I wrote enough articles about an aged ex-con named Pete Pianezzi to shame Gov. Jerry Brown into giving him a pardon based on innocence, one of only seven such pardons in the state's history. Pianezzi had been framed for a sensational Los Angeles mob hit of the 1930s that was page-one news up and down the West Coast. There were no good suspects, but Pianezzi was Italian, he had a criminal record, and the district attorney needed a conviction to quell the public pressure on his office. The prosecutor sought the death penalty, but a lone woman juror spared Pianezzi's life by refusing to vote for execution. She reportedly explained her hesitation by saying that if it turned out the jury was making a mistake—the defendant insisted at trial that he was innocent—that error could be reversed if Pianezzi were in prison, but not if he had gone to the gas chamber. This was a prescient observation. Forty years later, at a victory party in San Francisco, Pete introduced Standefer and me to the North Beach crowd as his "saviors," a distinction that properly belonged to that holdout juror whose name has been lost to posterity. She is the person who prevented the state from killing an innocent man.

To me, the most disturbing aspect of the Pianezzi case is that it was such a high-profile murder trial. If it can happen there, what about the anonymous cases in, for example, East Texas, in which the defendant is lucky if a news reporter ever sits through a whole day of testimony? Moreover, the Pianezzi case is no isolated example. Doubt about the guilt of the condemned man is a common thread in some of the most celebrated murder trials in this nation's history. Bruno Richard Hauptmann's chances for a fair trial in the Lindbergh kidnapping—and the ability truly to ascertain his guilt or innocence—were compromised by perjured testimony, tampering with exhibits, and the suppression by the New Jersey state police of exculpatory evidence. People remember also that Cleveland doctor Sam Sheppard's guilty verdict was set aside because of the circus-like atmosphere of the courtroom and the shameful conduct of Cleveland's newspapers. But do they recall that he was acquitted at his second trial?

The hardest questions

Conservatives were rightly appalled when O.J. Simpson was acquitted after a screwy trial tainted by the defense's overtly racial appeals to the jury. But the moral of this story is not that black jurors will no longer convict black defendants (of the 3,652 people on Death Row, 43 percent are black), it's that juries make mistakes all the time. And sometimes—nobody knows how often—the mistakes they make are in the other direction: They convict innocent people.

In the years since Steven T. Judy was electrocuted, some 82 condemned people have had their capital-murder convictions set aside for one reason or another. A few, such as Steven Manning, a corrupt Chicago cop, didn't get a fair trial but may have been guilty and are serving time for other crimes in which their guilt is unquestioned. But many more are like poor Kirk Bloodsworth, an ex-Marine from the Eastern Shore of Maryland who had no previous criminal record—and no involvement whatsoever in the crime for which he was convicted and sentenced to death. These men are released after years on Death Row with a pardon or a half-hearted apology by the state and, if they are lucky, an inadequate monetary settlement.

"I was separated from my family and branded the worst thing possible—a child-killer and a rapist," said Bloodsworth on his release. "It can happen to anyone."

In eight of these cases, including Bloodsworth's, DNA evidence not previously available was used to free the condemned. Inevitably someone on the prosecution's side will mumble bromides about how this proves that the system "works." But that's not what it proves. These DNA cases underscore a few basic points that are far from reassuring: What about the majority of cases—the non-rape cases, mostly—in which DNA is irrelevant? Why do so many state prosecutors tout DNA as much stronger evidence than fingerprints when it points to guilt, but then put up roadblocks for defendants who want to use it to establish their innocence? Finally, how many innocent people were executed in the years before DNA tests became available?

This is the crux of the matter, and no one seems to have the answer. Republican presidential candidate George W. Bush was asked directly how he could be certain that all 120-odd executions he has presided over as governor of Texas were carried out against guilty defendants. He replied that he was, indeed, certain that nothing like what had happened in Illinois had happened in Texas on his watch. "Maybe they've had some problems in their courts," he said. "Maybe they've had some faulty judgments. I've reviewed every case, . . . and I'm confident that every case that has come across my desk, I'm confident of the guilt of the person who committed the crime."

Incidentally, Bush's brother Jeb, the governor of Florida, says the same thing, even though Florida has set aside the capital-murder convictions of some 20 Death Row inmates since 1973—more than any other state. Gerald Kogan, the former chief justice of Florida's Supreme Court, entered the debate recently, saying he's convinced that Florida has, in fact, put to death people who were not guilty. "Knowing as I do the imperfections in our system, I know that we have, on occasions in the past, executed those people who are in fact innocent," Kogan said at a Capitol Hill press conference. This led, in turn, to a challenge from Jeb Bush that Kogan name names. This is a fair point, but present-day Florida officials hardly seem preoccupied with ensuring that only the guilty are put to death. When Gov. Ryan was imposing his moratorium, the legislature in Tallahassee was in special session passing a law reducing the time convicted murderers have to appeal their cases or bring new evidence to light.

If Republican governors are at odds with one another over the issue, so too are conservatives generally. Recently, Pat Robertson, George Will, and William F. Buckley Jr. have weighed in with op-ed pieces that express reservations about the death penalty over this matter of DNA and innocence.

I do not share George W. Bush's easy confidence that all of [the executed] were guilty.

Byron York, writing in *The American Spectator*, takes a different tack, arguing that innocence is a Trojan horse being used by liberals to advance a cause they have championed since the days of Darrow—abolition of capital punishment on the typical grounds: barbarism, racism, etc. The energetic Death Penalty Information Center in Washington, D.C., York points out, is virtually a wholly owned subsidiary of John R. "Rick" MacArthur, a rich left-winger whose taste in causes includes the Sandinistas and the Christic Institute.

York makes a valid point, and, as if to underscore it, all the usual suspects on the left have weighed in against capital punishment by simply topping their old arguments with a fresh concern about the risk of executing the innocent. In Hollywood, the writers of *The Practice*, a TV show concerning the law, turn one of their episodes into an anti-capital-punishment screed. From Chicago, Democratic representative Jesse Jackson Jr. authors a death-penalty-moratorium bill in the House. In Washington, Jackson's father, wearing one of his many hats as a CNN newsman—he hosts a show called *Both Sides,* a title Fidel Castro must love—interviews defense lawyer Barry Scheck, and no one else, about his book on condemned men who have been proven innocent by DNA. At one point in the decidedly one-sided program, Jackson invokes the memory of Supreme Court justice Harry Blackmun, who famously wrote in a 1994 dissent, "From this day forward, I no longer shall tinker with the machinery of death. I feel morally and intellectually obligated simply to concede that the death penalty has failed." Jackson and his lone guest keep using that word "moral" throughout the show, and the good reverend closes with the line "Let's choose life over death, but through it all, at least let's give life a chance."

In sum, it's enough to make any good conservative gag. Who wants to be on the same side as the Hollywood Left, or the two Jesse Jacksons, or Blackmun, the champion of life who wrote the *Roe* decision, or, for that matter, Barry Scheck, who attempted to convince the O.J. jury that DNA testing was a bunch of white man's mumbo-jumbo? The answer is that conservatives need to ignore their impulse that anything the liberal establishment approves of, they must oppose. They should instead focus on this one issue: If a democratic society executes criminals with the foreknowledge that some percentage of them are innocent, are all members of that society implicitly guilty of murder themselves? And does it matter, from a moral and theological viewpoint, that we can't know which convicts, specifically, will go to their deaths for crimes they did not commit, if we admit that some will? I submit that it does not.

The agony of doubt

Interviewed for a comprehensive piece published in November 1999 in *The Atlantic Monthly,* Bill McCollum, a conservative Republican congressman from Florida, suggested that the possibility of executing an innocent person—he insists it's a remote likelihood—is the price the nation must pay if it wants to reduce violent crime. In that same article, Chicago prosecutor William Kunkle, who secured the death penalty for serial killer John Wayne Gacy and also charged the police officers for their conduct in the Rolando Cruz case, went even further. He argued that anyone who believes man can design and implement a system that catches only the guilty is kidding himself. "Sooner or later it's going to happen," Kunkle said. "It comes with the territory. It is not humanly possible to design a system that is perfect. And if people are not prepared for the eventuality that human institutions are going to make mistakes, then they shouldn't support the death penalty, and they shouldn't elect legislators who support it."

Amen, Mr. Kunkle. Murder is a terrible crime. And in the face of the awful truth presented to us by DNA testing, what name shall we call the state-sanctioned killing of an innocent man? That's why society must not be a party to it. As Benjamin Franklin once said, "They that give up essential liberty to obtain a little temporary safety deserve neither liberty nor safety."

In 1982, a small-time Mexican-American thug named Leonel Torres Herrera was convicted of murdering two South Texas police officers. Herrera was sentenced to death. Eight years later, on the verge of his execution, a lawyer signed an affidavit saying that Herrera's brother had confessed the killings. Texas courts refused to reopen the case because the new assertion had come long after their 30-day limit for additional evidence. Herrera's case went all the way to the U.S. Supreme Court, which ruled 6 to 3 that Texas's time limitations were not unconstitutional. The case sharply divided the high court. Justice Blackmun said caustically from the bench that "the execution of a person who can show that he is innocent comes perilously close to simple murder." Sandra Day O'Connor, looking at other evidence in the case, replied in her written opinion that Herrera was not innocent "in any sense of the word."

O'Connor's clear-eyed observation should not be forgotten. Most of the time, the condemned are guilty. I certainly hope she is right in the Herrera case. But I am haunted by the possibility, no matter how remote, that she isn't. In the two decades since Steven Judy went to his richly deserved death, 631 others have been executed. I do not share George W. Bush's easy confidence that all of them were guilty. In 1981, the same year that Judy died and Leonel Herrera was apprehended, Pete Pianezzi was pardoned. Pete, then a very old man, told me when he got the news that he never really despaired that he would someday be vindicated because innocence, like truth, exists as a power of its own in the world, independent of the machinations of men. Pete died a few years ago, but his faith was greater than mine. Only God—not any living man—knows, for instance, whether Leonel Herrera really did it. All we know for sure is what the condemned man himself said as he left this world.

"Something very wrong is taking place tonight," he cried. "I am innocent, innocent, innocent . . ."

9

The Possibility of Wrongful Executions Does Not Justify Abolishing the Death Penalty

Samuel Francis

Samuel Francis is a contributing editor of Chronicles, *a monthly conservative journal.*

Responding to claims that innocent prisoners might be sentenced to death and executed, conservatives as well as liberals have increasingly called for the suspension or the abolition of capital punishment. However, there is no proof that any innocent people have been executed in recent years. Furthermore, the argument that the state should not execute unless it can be certain that no innocents are put to death is dubious. There is no way to ensure absolute certainty in human reasoning. If perfect certainty were required in criminal justice matters, then even life imprisonment should be abolished because innocents might receive such sentences. The whims of politicians and activists who question the administration of the death penalty should not be allowed to usurp judicial authority.

"Well, fellow, who are you?" demands the Earl of Warwick of a character who appears on stage for the first time at the end of George Bernard Shaw's play *Saint Joan*. "I," huffs the man who has just burned Joan of Arc at the stake, "am not addressed as fellow, my lord. I am the Master Executioner of Rouen: It is a highly skilled mystery."

In the more civilized times of the late Middle Ages, the art and science of putting people to death was indeed a highly skilled mystery, much like the manufacture of stained glass or the embalming of mummies, and both rulers and ruled took pride in the craftsmen whose profession it was to mete out torture and death to convicted criminals. Contrary to Hollywood myth, executioners seldom wore hoods or masks, for the simple reason that no one saw anything wrong, shameful, or disreputable in how they made their living. Indeed, whole families spawned generations of professional executioners (the Sanson family of France was the best known). The only occasion that I know of on which an executioner wore a mask was at the judicial murder of King Charles I of England in 1649, and both the headsman who wielded the ax and the more brutal killers who engineered the king's decapitation had good reason to be both ashamed and afraid of what they were doing. But ordinarily, when real criminals and traitors mounted the scaffold, it occurred to no one to hide or try to minimize the supreme act of solemn justice that took place in a legal execution.

Executions under attack

Today, however, executions are virtually state secrets, performed during the night at hidden locations deep within prison walls, witnessed only by a handful of journalists and other perverts who have enough clout with the governor to get a seat at the proceedings, and carried out not by men who take pride in what they do, but by nameless state troopers and prison guards forced to draw lots for the duty. Even these evasions aren't enough: Executions themselves are now disguised as medical operations, planned to be as painless and unfrightening as possible, lest the poor little murderers and rapists who have to get a jolt of hot juice might be intimidated at the last minute. Some years ago, when the state of Texas pioneered lethal injection as a method of capital punishment, lawmakers tried to force prison doctors to carry it out. The doctors, to their credit, simply refused, citing the Hippocratic oath that forbids them to take human life and insisting that the state acknowledge that executions are not just somewhat more elaborate tonsillectomies.

There is no evidence whatsoever that, in recent years, any innocent person has been executed.

Recently, however, even the nearly bloodless executions we still carry out have come under attack: from the United Nations and its army of "human rights" watchers; from the Pope, who helped spring a convicted murderer in Missouri a few years ago; and from "conservatives"—namely, Pat Robertson, George Will, and William F. Buckley, Jr., as well as the moderate Republican governor of Illinois [George H. Ryan], who has suspended further executions in his state until he can be certain that their guests of honor are really guilty. Mr. Buckley's magazine, *National Review*, which still claims to be the major conservative journal of opinion in the country, ran a long article arguing against the death penalty in its June 19, 2000, issue. The article, by Carl M. Cannon, was subtitled "a conservative case against capital punishment," although there was nothing conservative about Mr. Cannon's argument. The same issue sported an editorial entitled "Thou shalt not fry," which, as *National Review* editorials in recent years have often done, failed to tell the readers what to think about the matter.

"Advances in forensic techniques ensure that wrongful convictions will continue to be exposed," the editorial bleated. "This raises political, intellectual, and moral questions that conservatives must address."

The "advances in forensic techniques" are, in fact, the major causes of all the reconsiderations of the death penalty by people who have been and ought still to be in favor of it. The possibility of DNA testing now allows the police and the courts to determine whether some defendants or convicts are really the same individuals who left their hair, blood, saliva, semen, or skin cells at a crime scene. In Illinois, for example, some 13 chaps condemned to death have been exonerated of their capital crimes during the past two decades, though only in part because of DNA tests, and it was this fact that Governor Ryan, in January 2000, used as justification for suspending further executions. "Until I can be sure that everyone sentenced to death in Illinois is truly guilty; until I can be sure, with moral certainty, that no innocent man or woman is facing a lethal injection, no one will meet that fate," the governor intoned. And much the same sentiment seems to guide the thoughts of the other conservative gurus who have changed their minds or are entertaining doubts about the death penalty.

An argument without merit

That also is the brunt of Mr. Cannon's argument in *National Review*. Pointing to his experience in invalidating the convictions of condemned criminals, as well as to the 82 known cases of capital convictions since 1981 that have been "set aside for one reason or another" (not necessarily, be it noted, because innocence has been proved, though the author rather leaves the reader with that impression), Mr. Cannon insists that innocent people have certainly been executed and that "the right question to ask is . . . whether the government should be in the business of executing people convicted of murder knowing to a certainty that some of them are innocent."

That, essentially, is also the argument advanced by Buckley, Robertson, and Will, and it is entirely without merit. Note, first of all, that Mr. Cannon claims to be arguing that a convict shouldn't be executed unless we are certain he's guilty, which is reasonable. But what he actually says in the sentence quoted above is that the state is executing people it is certain are innocent. Not only are the two claims quite different, but there is no evidence whatsoever that, in recent years, any innocent person has been executed (let alone that state authorities knew for a certainty he was innocent). Neither Mr. Cannon nor anyone else even claims that it's so—except by inference. Because some people condemned to death in recent years have been shown to be innocent, therefore some people who were executed were also innocent. That may be true, but it doesn't follow, and it hasn't been established.

Moreover, if DNA testing proves innocence in some cases, in others it ought to prove guilt, an implication that blows the argument about "certainty" out of the water. The argument is that, as Governor Ryan says, until we "can be sure, with moral certainty," that no innocent person is being executed, we should have no executions. But what if we are certain he is guilty? If the "conservative case against capital punishment" applies only to innocent people wrongly condemned to death, then it's not an argument against capital punishment but an argument against executing innocent people, which no one questions.

"Certainty" is rare

As for "certainty" itself, the governor, Mr. Cannon, and some of the other critics invoke it casually. The fact is that "certainty," in the sense they are using the word, is rarely available in contested criminal proceedings or any other human judgment. The standard in American courts of law is that guilt must be proved "beyond a reasonable doubt," but that is not the "certainty" the critics demand. In Maryland in the summer of 2000, liberal Democratic Gov. Parris Glendening commuted the death sentence of a man named Eugene Colvin-el, who was convicted of a 1980 murder in which his bloody fingerprint was found at the crime scene. The convict was also known to have pawned a pocket watch belonging to the victim. In commuting the sentence, Governor Glendening said, "I believe that Colvin-el committed this crime, but I do not have the same level of absolute certainty" as in other cases. If Colvin-el's DNA had been found on the victim instead of his fingerprint, would that have established "certainty" for the governor? By this standard, you have to wonder how anyone can ever know anything. The standard of "certainty" collapses into epistemological nihilism.

Yet I venture to guess that if someone else's fingerprint had been found at the crime scene, that would have been taken as certain proof of Colvin-el's innocence. Mr. Cannon, as well as Governors Ryan and Glendening, seem to have no problem with "certainty" when it points to innocence and gets somebody off Death Row; it's only when everyone else—police, prosecutors, judges, and juries—is certain of guilt that they invoke doubt.

In any case, it is not the business of a governor, in Illinois or Maryland, conservative or liberal, to second-guess the courts. The reason we have courts at all is to establish what Governors Ryan and Glendening insist on deciding for themselves. If the governors have good reason to believe condemned men have been wrongfully or unfairly convicted (through new evidence or reviews of trials and appeals), then commutations, reprieves, or pardons may be in order. But to overturn what the courts have already determined through due process simply because it doesn't conform to the governors' private whims is a usurpation of judicial authority.

> *Certainty . . . is rarely available in contested criminal proceedings or any other human judgment.*

Of course, innocent people may well have been executed. Mr. Cannon mentions the case of Bruno Hauptmann, executed in 1936 for the murder of the Lindbergh baby, and there is good reason to believe Hauptmann was railroaded to his death by the state of New Jersey (particularly by the head of the New Jersey state police at the time, a gentleman named

Norman Schwarzkopf, father of the general glamorized in the Gulf War. Slaughtering innocent people may run in the family blood, much as killing criminals ran in the blood of the Sanson clan). As Mr. Cannon acknowledges, errors happen, and sometimes, as we all know from the novels of Raymond Chandler and James Ellroy, the cops or prosecutors pick a guy for the fall simply because he looks good for it, not because there's any real evidence.

> *No matter how advanced forensic techniques become, there is always going to be an element of uncertainty in some cases . . . just as there always has been.*

But these are not flaws of the system of punishment. They are, at most, flaws of the law-enforcement and judicial systems or of human nature itself, and if government is going to be halted by them, it's not clear what it can do. If the criminal justice system is convicting innocent people, should it impose any punishment at all? Mr. Cannon speaks of the waste experienced by wrongfully convicted men "released after years on Death Row with a pardon or a half-hearted apology by the state and, if they are lucky, an inadequate monetary settlement." Of course, the same could be said of innocent men sentenced to life imprisonment. Given the critics' certainty of uncertainty, it's hard to see how you could cross the street without being smacked by a truck.

The collapse of moral certainty

None of the arguments against capital punishment mounted by conservatives is very new, and none is particularly compelling. No matter how advanced forensic techniques become, there is always going to be an element of uncertainty in some cases, perhaps in all cases, just as there always has been. What the new conservative "case against capital punishment" really proves is not the injustice or inexpediency of the death penalty, but the disintegration of the conservative mind and its digestion by the omnivorous mentality of the left, to the point that it is no longer distinguishable from the latter.

"The age is running mad after innovation," Samuel Johnson remarked to Sir William Scott when he learned that the procession of condemned prisoners from Newgate jail to Tyburn tree was to be abolished, "and all the business of the world is to be done in a new way; men are to be hanged in a new way; Tyburn itself is not safe from the fury of innovation." Dr. Johnson was not a cruel man, and it's doubtful he took any pleasure in the executions that served as spectator sport in the England of his time, but he saw in the abolition of the procession of the damned an ominous symbol of what was coming: a creeping uncertainty about good and evil, right and wrong, justice and injustice, and reward and punishment that at first infected only those of his own contemporaries who were most furious for innovation, but which eventually would spread to those who are supposed to be immune to it. The consequence of the collapse of moral certainty is an unwillingness to assert moral authority of any kind or to back it up by the use of force, whether it involves merely the spanking of children or the highly skilled mystery of executing criminals, and the collapse and its consequences have been evident in the mentality of the left ever since Dr. Johnson's day, to the point that they now threaten the survival of civilization itself. What the "conservative" case against capital punishment shows is that the collapse is no longer confined to the mind of the left but has captured a major beachhead within the mind of the right as well. That capture confirms, once again, that the right, as it has been known for the last half century, no longer exists except as an appendage of the left, and that it can no longer serve as a useful instrument of resistance to leftist demands.

10

Effective Legal Counsel and DNA Testing Could Prevent the Execution of Innocents

Patrick Leahy

Patrick Leahy is the Democratic senator from Vermont.

Since the reinstatement of capital punishment in the United States in 1976, at least eighty-five inmates have been found innocent and have had their death sentences overturned. It is highly likely that wrongly convicted people have been executed. This serious crisis in the application of the death penalty is the result of a governmental unwillingness to ensure that defendants receive competent legal assistance and opportunities to be vindicated by postconviction evidence. States should be required to provide capital defendants with adequate legal representation, and inmates should be granted genuine opportunities to claim innocence on the basis of DNA tests and other kinds of potentially exonerating evidence. It behooves both the critics and supporters of the death penalty to find ways to prevent the execution of innocents—the ultimate miscarriage of justice.

I wish to call attention to a growing national crisis in the administration of capital punishment. People of good conscience can and will disagree on the morality of the death penalty. But I am confident that we should all be able to agree that a system that may sentence one innocent person to death for every seven it executes has no place in a civilized society, much less in 21st century America. But that is what the American system of capital punishment has done since 1976.

More than 600 have been executed since the reinstatement of capital punishment in 1976. During the same time, according to the Death Penalty Information Center at least 85 people have been found innocent and were released from death row. These are not reversals of sentences, or even convictions on technical legal grounds; these are people whose convictions have been overturned after years of confinement on death row

Patrick Leahy, "The Growing Crisis in the Administration of Capital Punishment," *The Congressional Record*, February 1, 2002, p. S198.

because it was discovered they were not guilty. Even though in some instances they came within hours of being executed, it was eventually determined that, whoops, we made a mistake; we have the wrong person.

What does this mean? It means that for every seven executions, one person has been wrongly convicted. It means that we could have more than three innocent people sentenced to death each year. The phenomenon is not confined to just a few states; the many exonerations since 1976 span more than 20 different states. And of those who are found innocent—not released because of a technicality, but actually found innocent—what is the average time they spent on death row, knowing they could be executed at any time? What is the average time they spent on death row before somebody said, we have the wrong person? Seven and a half years.

A system that may sentence one innocent person to death for every seven it executes has no place in a civilized society.

This would be disturbing enough if the eventual exonerations of these death row inmates were the product of reliable and consistent checks in our legal system, if we could say as Americans, all right, you may spend 7½ years on death row, but at least you have the comfort of knowing that we are going to find out you are innocent before we execute you. It might be comprehensible, though not acceptable, if we as a society lacked effective and relatively inexpensive means to make capital punishment more reliable. But many of the exonerated owe their lives to fortuity and private heroism, having been denied commonsense procedural rights and inexpensive modern scientific testing opportunities—leaving open the very real possibility that there have been a number of innocent people executed over the last few decades who were not so fortunate.

Sample cases

Let me give you a case. Randall Dale Adams. Here is a man who might have been routinely executed had his case not attracted the attention of a filmmaker, Earl Morris. His movie, *The Thin Blue Line*, shredded the prosecution's case and cast a national spotlight on Adams' innocence.

Consider the case of Anthony Porter. Porter spent 16 years on death row. That is more years than most Members of the Senate have served. He spent 16 years on death row. He came within 48 hours of being executed in 1998, but he was cleared the following year. Was he cleared by the state? No. He was cleared by a class of undergraduate journalism students at Northwestern University, who took on his case as a class project. That got him out. Then the State acknowledged that it had the wrong person, that Porter had been innocent all along. He came within 48 hours of being executed, and he would have been executed had not this journalism class decided to investigate his case instead of doing something else. Now consider the cases of the unknown and the unlucky, about whom we may never hear.

In 1999, former Florida Supreme Court Justice Gerald Kogan said he had 'no question' that 'we certainly have, in the past, executed . . . people who either didn't fit the criteria for execution in the State of Florida, or who, in fact, were, factually, not guilty of the crime for which they have been executed.' This is not some pie-in-the-sky theory. Justice Kogan was a homicide detective and a prosecutor before eventually rising to Chief Justice.

This crisis has led the American Bar Association and a growing number of State legislators to call for a moratorium on executions until the death penalty can be administered with less risk to the innocent. In January 2000, the Republican Governor of Illinois, George Ryan, announced he plans to block executions in that State until an inquiry has been conducted into why more death row inmates have been exonerated than executed since 1977 when Illinois reinstated capital punishment. Think of that. More death row inmates exonerated than executed.

Governor Ryan is someone who supports the death penalty. But I agree with him in bringing this halt. He said: 'There is a flaw in the system, without question, and it needs to be studied.' The governor is absolutely right. I rise to bring to this body [the Senate] the debate over how we as a nation can begin to reduce the risk of killing the innocent.

Addressing the crisis

I hope that nobody of good faith—whether they are for or against the death penalty—will deny the existence of a serious crisis. Sentencing innocent women and men to death anywhere in our country shatters America's image in the international community. At the very least, it undermines our leadership in the struggle for human rights. But, more importantly, the individual and collective conscience of decent Americans is deeply offended and the faith in the working of our criminal justice system is severely damaged. So the question we should debate is, what should be done?

Some will be tempted to rely on the states. The U.S. Supreme Court often defers to "the laboratory of the states" to figure out how to protect criminal defendants. After a quarter of a century, let's take a look at that lab report.

As I already mentioned, Illinois has now had more inmates released from death row than executed since the death penalty was reinstated. There have been 12 executions, and 13 times they have said: Whoops, sorry. Don't pull the switch. We have the wrong person. This has happened four times in 1999 alone.

We could have more than three innocent people sentenced to death each year.

In Texas, the state that leads the nation in executions, courts have upheld death sentences in at least three cases in which the defense lawyers slept through substantial portions of the trial. The Texas courts said that the defendants in these cases had adequate counsel. Adequate counsel?

Would any one of us if we were in a taxicab say we had an adequate driver who was asleep at the wheel? What we are saying is with a person's life at stake the defense lawyer slept through the trial, and the Texas courts say that is pretty adequate.

Meanwhile, in the past few years, the states have followed the federal lead in expanding their defective capital punishment systems, curtailing appeal and habeas corpus rights, and slashing funding for indigent defense services. The crisis can only get worse.

[In 1993, the Supreme Court] could not even make up its mind whether the execution of an innocent person would be unconstitutional.

The states have had decades to fix their capital punishment systems, yet the best they have managed is a system fraught with arbitrariness and error—a system where innocent people are sentenced to death on a regular basis, and it is left not to the courts, not to the states, not to the federal government, but to filmmakers and college undergraduates to correct the mistakes. History shows that we cannot rely on local politics to implement our national conscience on such fundamental points as the execution of the innocent.

What about the Supreme Court? In a 1993 case, it could not even make up its mind whether the execution of an innocent person would be unconstitutional. Do a referendum on that one throughout the Nation. Ask people in this nation of a quarter billion people whether they think executing an innocent person should be considered constitutional or unconstitutional. Most in this country have no doubt that it would be unconstitutional, but that really does not matter: executing an innocent person is abhorrent—it is morally wrong. Whether you support the death penalty or not, executing an innocent person is wrong, and we in this body have the moral duty to express and implement America's conscience. We should be the nation's conscience. The buck should stop in this chamber where it always stops in times of national crisis.

How do we begin to stem the crisis? I have been posing this question to experts across the country for nearly a year. There is a lot of consensus over what must be done. In the next few weeks, I will introduce legislation that will address some of the most urgent problems in the administration of capital punishment.

Two problems in particular require our immediate attention. First, we need to ensure that defendants in capital cases receive competent legal representation at every stage in their case. Second, we have to guarantee an effective forum for death row inmates who may be able to prove their innocence.

The need for effective counsel

In our adversarial system of justice, effective assistance of counsel is essential to the fair administration of justice. It is the principal bulwark against wrongful conviction.

I know this from my own experience as a prosecutor. It is the best way to reduce the risk that a trial will be infected by constitutional error, resulting in reversal, retrial, cost, delay, and repeated ordeals for the victim's family. Most prosecutors will tell you they would much prefer to have good counsel on the other side because there is less apt to be mistakes, there is less apt to be reversible error, and there is far more of a chance that you end up with the right decision.

Most defendants who face capital charges are represented by court-appointed lawyers. Unfortunately, the manner in which defense lawyers are selected and compensated in death penalty cases frequently fails to protect the defendant's rights. Some states relegate these cases to grossly unqualified lawyers willing to settle for meager fees. While the federal government pays defense counsel $125 an hour for death penalty work, the hourly rate in many States is $50 or less, and some states place an arbitrary and usually unrealistically low cap on the total amount a court-appointed attorney can bill.

New York recently slashed pay for counsel in capital cases by as much as 50 percent. They might say they are getting their money's worth if they cut out all the money for defense counsel. The conviction rate is probably going to shoot up. Let me tell you what else will go up—the number of innocent people who will be put to death.

> *[States] should not be permitted to tip the scales of justice by denying capital defendants competent legal services.*

Congress has done its part to make a bad situation worse. In 1996, Congress defunded the death penalty resource centers. This has sharply increased the chances that innocent persons will be executed.

You get what you pay for. Those who are on death row have found their lives placed in the hands of lawyers who are drunk during the trial—in some instances, lawyers who never bothered to meet their client before the trial; lawyers who never bothered to read the state death penalty statute; lawyers who were just out of law school and never handled a criminal case; and lawyers who were literally asleep on the job.

Even some of our best lawyers, diligent, experienced litigators, can do little when they lack funds for investigators, experts, or scientific testing that could establish their client's innocence. Attorneys appointed to represent capital defendants often cannot recoup even their out-of-pocket expenses. They are effectively required to work at minimum wage or below while funding their client's defense out of their own pockets.

Although the states are required to provide criminal defendants with qualified legal counsel, those who have been saved from death row and found innocent were often convicted because of attorney error. They might not have had postconviction review because their lawyer failed to meet a filing deadline. An attorney misses a deadline by even 1 day, and his death row client may pay the price with his life.

Let me be clear what I am talking about. I am not suggesting that there is a universal right to Johnnie Cochran's services. The O.J. Simpson case has absolutely nothing to do with the typical capital case, in which one or possibly two underfunded and underprepared lawyers try to cobble together a defense with little or no scientific or expert evidence and the whole process takes less than a week. These are two extremes. You go from the Simpson case, where the judge let the whole thing get out of control and we had a year-long spectacle, to the typical death penalty case which is rushed through without preparation in a matter of days. Somewhere there must be a middle ground.

Let me give three examples of some of the worst things that have happened—but not untypical.

Ronald Keith Williamson. In 1997, a Federal appeals court overturned Williamson's conviction on the basis of ineffectiveness of counsel. The court noted that the lawyer, who had been paid a total of $3,200 for the defense, had failed to investigate and present a fact to the jury. What was that fact? Somebody else confessed to the crime. If I were the defense attorney, I think one of the things that I would want to bring to the jury is the fact that somebody else confessed to the crime; Williamson's lawyer did not bother. Then, two years after the appeals court decision, DNA testing ruled out Williamson as the killer and implicated another man—a convicted kidnapper who had testified against Williamson at trial. Of course, he did. He is the one who committed the crime.

The case of George McFarland

Let's next consider George McFarland. According to the Texas Court of Criminal Appeals, McFarland's lawyer slept through much of his 1992 trial. He objected to hardly anything the prosecution did. Here is how the *Houston Chronicle* described what happened as McFarland stood on trial for his life. This is not for shoplifting. He is on trial for his life.

Let me quote from the *Houston Chronicle*:

> Seated beside his client . . . defense attorney John Benn spent much of Thursday afternoon's trial in apparent deep sleep. His mouth kept falling open and his head lolled back on his shoulders, and then he awakened just long enough to catch himself and sit upright. Then it happened again. And again. And again.

> Every time he opened his eyes, a different prosecution witness was on the stand describing another aspect of the Nov. 19, 1991, arrest of George McFarland in the robbery-killing of grocer Kenneth Kwan.

> When state District Judge Doug Shaver finally called a recess, Benn was asked if he truly had fallen asleep during a capital murder trial. 'It's boring,' the 72-year-old longtime Houston lawyer explained. . . . Court observers said Benn seems to have slept his way through virtually the entire trial.

Unfortunately for McFarland, Texas' highest criminal court, several of whose members were coming up for reelection, concluded that this constituted effective criminal representation.

I guess they felt because the lawyer was in the courtroom, even though sound asleep, that would be effective representation. If you read the decision they probably would have ruled the same way if he had been at home sound asleep, so long as he had been appointed at some time.

Improvements in DNA testing have exposed the fallibility of the legal system.

McFarland is still on death row for a murder he insists he did not commit, on the basis of evidence widely reported by independent observers to be weak.

Then we have Reginald Powell, a borderline mentally retarded man who was 18 at the time of the crime. Mr. Powell was eventually executed. Why? Because he accepted his lawyer's advice to reject a plea bargain that would have saved his life.

There were a number of attorney errors at the trial. The advice he received seems to be very bad advice. Some may feel this advice, the advice given to this 18-year-old mentally retarded man, was affected by the flagrantly unprofessional conduct of the attorney, a woman twice Powell's age, who conducted a secret jailhouse sexual relationship with him during the trial. Despite this obvious attorney conflict of interest, Powell's execution went ahead in Missouri in 1999.

I ask each Member of the Senate when you go home tonight, or when you talk to your constituents, and when you consider the bill I will be introducing, to remember these cases and consult your conscience to ask whether these examples represent the best of 21st century American justice.

The judge who presided over McFarland's trial summed up the Texas court's view of the law quite accurately when he reasoned that, while the Constitution requires a defendant to be represented by a lawyer, it 'doesn't say the lawyer has to be awake.' If your conscience says otherwise, maybe we ought to do something.

My proposal rests on a simple premise: States that choose to impose capital punishment must be prepared to foot the bill. They should not be permitted to tip the scales of justice by denying capital defendants competent legal services. We have to do everything we can to ensure the states are meeting their constitutional obligations with respect to capital representation.

Postconviction evidence

Can miscarriages of justice happen when defendants receive adequate representation? Yes, they can still happen. So I think it is critical to ensure that death row inmates have a meaningful opportunity—not a fanciful opportunity but a meaningful opportunity—to raise claims of innocence based on newly discovered evidence, especially if it is evidence that is derived from scientific tests not available at the time of the trial.

Perhaps more than any other development, improvements in DNA testing have exposed the fallibility of the legal system. In the last decades, scores of wrongfully convicted people have been released from prison—including many from death row—after DNA testing proved they could not have committed the crimes for which they were convicted. In some cases the same DNA testing that vindicated the innocent helped catch the guilty.

Most recently, DNA testing exonerated Ronald Jones. He spent close to 8 years on death row for a 1985 rape and murder that he did not commit. Illinois prosecutors dropped the charges against Jones on May 18, 1999, after DNA evidence from the crime scene excluded him as a possible suspect.

It was also DNA testing that eventually saved Ronald Keith Williamson's life, as I discussed earlier. He spent 12 years as an innocent man on Oklahoma's death row.

Can you imagine how any one of us would feel, day after day for 12 years, never knowing if we were just a few hours or a few days from execution, locked up on death row for a crime we did not commit?

Some of the major hurdles to postconviction DNA testing are laws prohibiting introduction of new evidence—laws that have tightened as death penalty supporters have tried to speed executions by limiting appeals. Only two states, New York and Illinois, require the opportunity for inmates to require DNA testing where it could result in new evidence of innocence. Elsewhere, inmates may try to get DNA evidence for years, only to be shut out by courts and prosecutors.

The pursuit of justice obliges us not only to convict the guilty, but also to exonerate the wrongly accused and convicted.

What possible reason could there be to deny inmates the opportunity to prove their innocence—and perhaps even help identify the real culprits—through new technologies? DNA testing is relatively inexpensive. But no matter what it costs, it is a tiny price to pay to make sure you have the right person.

The National Commission on the Future of DNA Evidence, a federal panel established by the Justice Department and comprised of law enforcement, judicial, and scientific experts, issued a report in 1999 urging prosecutors to consent to postconviction DNA testing, or retesting, in appropriate cases, especially if the results could exonerate the defendant.

In 1994, we set up a funding program to improve the quality and availability of DNA analysis for law enforcement identification purposes. The Justice Department has handed out tens of millions of dollars to States under this program. In 1999 alone, we appropriated another $30 million for DNA-related grants to states. That is an appropriate use of federal funds. But we should not pass up the promise of truth and justice for both sides of our adversarial system that DNA evidence holds out. We at least ought to require that both sides have it available.

By reexamining capital punishment in light of recent exonerations, we can reduce the risk that people will be executed for crimes they did not commit and increase the probability that the guilty will be brought to justice. We can also help to make sure the death penalty is not imposed out of ignorance or prejudice.

I learned, first as a defense attorney and then as a prosecutor, that the pursuit of justice obliges us not only to convict the guilty, but also to exonerate the wrongly accused and convicted. That obligation is all the more urgent when the death penalty is involved.

Let's not have the situation where, today in America, it is better to be rich and guilty than poor and innocent. That is not equal justice. That is not what our country stands for.

I was proud to be a defense attorney. I was very proud to be a prosecutor. I have often said it was probably the best job I ever had. But there was one thought I always had every day that I was a prosecutor. I would look at the evidence over and over again and I would ask myself, not can I get a conviction on this charge, but will I be convicting the right person. I had cases where I knew I could get a conviction, but I believed we had the wrong person, and I would not bring the charge. I think most prosecutors feel that way. But sometimes in the passion of a highly publicized, horrendous murder, we can move too fast.

I urge Senators on both sides of the aisle, both those who support the death penalty and those who oppose it, to join in seeking ways to reduce the risk of mistaken executions.

11

DNA Evidence Will Not Prevent the Execution of Innocents

Philip Brasfield

Philip Brasfield is a contributing editor of The Other Side, *a progressive Christian journal. He is also the assistant executive director of the Lamp of Hope Project, an organization that advocates for the civil rights of prisoners, and an adviser to the Texas Coalition to Abolish the Death Penalty. He has been in prison for more than twenty years.*

The growing public awareness about wrongful convictions and the number of innocents who have been sentenced to death has changed the dynamics of the death-penalty debate. The use of postconviction DNA evidence, which has exonerated dozens of wrongly accused inmates, has helped to reveal the fallibility of the legal system. Many who promote the use of DNA evidence believe that it will enable law enforcement officials to track down real criminals faster and prevent wrongful executions. However, DNA tests are useless in cases where no evidence is found at the crime scene. Moreover, DNA evidence might allay concerns about wrongful applications of the death penalty and could ultimately create more support for capital punishment. The use of DNA evidence will not necessarily prevent the execution of innocents or lead to the abolition of the death penalty.

G ary Graham vowed to "fight them like hell!" and he did, for nearly two full decades. It did him no good. The state of Texas killed him in June of 2000, just as they'd planned.

Graham's hotly contested case was the latest high-profile cause célèbre on Texas's death row. His was the 222nd lethal injection since this state resumed executions in 1982; the 135th state killing overseen by George W. Bush, who still believes everyone ever executed in Texas was guilty.

Like the 1998 execution of Karla Faye Tucker, Graham's execution was accentuated by the macabre. Passionate demonstrators—both "for" and

Philip Brasfield, "The End of Innocence," *The Other Side*, vol. 36, December 2000, pp. 40–43. Copyright © 2000 by *The Other Side*. Reproduced by permission.

"against" the death penalty—created an eerie carnival-like atmosphere. Attending lawmen allowed the good ol' boys from the Ku Klux Klan to parade up and down one sequestered street, while members of the New Black Panther Party enjoyed some kind of Texas-style affirmative action as they marched along another blockaded street, then posed with unloaded weapons and mugged for the cameras. High-profile abolitionists like Jesse Jackson, Al Sharpton, and Bianca Jagger came to Huntsville, Texas. The media swarmed on the Walls Unit like a plague of high-tech locusts.

A few Saturdays later I asked a dozen friends and coworkers in this Texas prison if they remembered what had happened a month earlier in Huntsville that made worldwide news. Not a single person remembered.

How could even those of us in prison forget a case like Graham's so easily, so completely, so soon? And what of the majority of executions, in which the condemned die as they have lived—not so much in infamy but in social abandonment, cultural anonymity, and public silence?

A new struggle

The lives of those killed in our names are quickly forgotten once the crowds move on. But the debate over the death penalty is not the same struggle it has been for the past twenty years.

Without warning or fanfare, Republican governor George Ryan of Illinois declared an abrupt halt to his state's death machine in January 2000, after learning that thirteen men sentenced to death there since 1977 had been released when their innocence was proven by additional post-trial investigations. During that same period of time, twelve other men were executed in Illinois. "I have grave concerns about our state's shameful record of convicting innocent people," Ryan said. "There is no margin for error when it comes to putting a person to death."

Ryan's honesty seemed to be a catalyst that gave political permission to other lawmakers around the country. Moratorium campaigns are currently viable in Pennsylvania, Oklahoma, and Missouri. In Oregon, Kentucky, and New Hampshire, genuine grass-roots abolition initiatives have spread in state legislatures like wildfire. In Florida, where yet another Governor Bush is in power, Circuit Judge Robert P. Cates recently overturned the sentence of a man condemned to die in 1993, the twenty-first time a wrongful conviction and death sentence has been overturned in that state. Nationally, it marked the eighty-seventh reversal of a false conviction and death sentence since the death penalty was reinstated.

All the DNA tests in the world would not save [Gary Graham], for no evidence was left at the scene of the crime for which he was convicted.

The publication of *Actual Innocence: Five Days to Execution and Other Dispatches from the Wrongly Convicted,* by Jim Dwyer, Peter Neufeld, and Barry Scheck (Doubleday, 2000) further highlights the fallibility of our criminal system. *Actual Innocence* combines legal precedent, scholarly studies, case histories, research statistics, and anecdotal information to paint a vivid portrait of the issues surrounding the wrongful convictions of sixty-two men whose innocence was later conclusively proven through the use of DNA testing.

The authors of *Actual Innocence* don't hesitate to tell the truth about the underbelly of criminal trials: eyewitnesses make mistakes. Snitches lie. Confessions are forced, coerced, or fabricated. Lab tests are wrong and sometimes rigged. Racism asphyxiates the truth. Defense lawyers sleep or stagger drunk or stoned through trials. Prosecutors lie. (This is all common knowledge to those of us who have been through "the system," as well as to those who earn their living in it.)

Statistically, these factors have proven to make little difference to juries in death penalty cases, who return a guilty verdict and death sentence in more than 80 percent of cases in which prosecutors request this sentence. But the new information coming to light with the increasing use of DNA testing is severely compromising the system's presumption of guilt.

The impact of DNA evidence

Law-enforcement officials, prosecutors, judges, and defense lawyers all agree that the use of DNA evidence to determine guilt or innocence, particularly in rape and rape-murder cases, is changing the criminal-justice system. In fact, they believe the impact is just beginning to be felt.

A U.S. Department of Justice report states that police departments around the country now routinely send DNA samples to FBI labs for potential matching in most rape and rape-murder cases. In eighteen thousand cases where the DNA evidence was analyzed, forty-five hundred of the primary suspects have been exonerated—a 26 percent rate of error that might not have been discovered otherwise. The Justice Department's task force went on to question the validity of convictions obtained without benefit of DNA testing, stating that the "strong presumption that those verdicts are correct has been weakened."

More and more law-enforcement agencies are using the growing DNA database around the country to clear cases that have been unsolved for years. In June 1996, a Texas court sentenced a prisoner to life for two counts of aggravated assault solely on DNA evidence left at the scene of the crime. The evidence matched a sample in the state's DNA database— a "cold hit" of someone not suspected earlier of involvement in the crime. Five states have now filed "John Doe" cases against unknown rape suspects, preserving DNA evidence for trial in the event that suspects are uncovered after the statute of limitations expires.

And then there's Roy Criner. Criner was convicted of rape-murder in Montgomery County, Texas, twelve years ago and sentenced to a ninety-nine-year sentence. He has always maintained his innocence. Finally, in 1998, he was vindicated, when testing of DNA evidence from the crime scene revealed no connection to him. Yet the state refused to release him at that time, arguing that the failed match did not prove he didn't commit the crime. Criminal Appeals Judge Sharon Keller repeatedly rejected calls for a new trial, contending that the DNA proved nothing, since "everyone knew she slept around." Criner was finally freed on August 15 of 2000, having spent more than a decade in prison for a crime he didn't commit.

Meanwhile, in Smith County, Texas, A.B. Butler is also free, after serving sixteen years in prison for a 1983 rape he always insisted he didn't commit. Nobody in the criminal-justice system believed him, but DNA testing arranged by attorney Barry Scheck exonerated him.

A "magic bullet"?

Scheck believes DNA testing is a "magic bullet" that should be used in every case where it would make a difference. Not everyone agrees. The American Civil Liberties Union (ACLU) recently urged Congress to open their eyes to the unseen dangers posed by the government's growing zeal to create a DNA database of those suspected of violating the law.

"While DNA databases may be useful to identify criminals, I'm skeptical that we will ward off the temptation to expand their use," said Barry Steinhardt, associate director of the ACLU. "In the last ten years we've moved from collecting DNA only from convicted sex offenders to including people who've been arrested but never convicted of a crime. There have even been proposals to store the DNA of newborn children for future use by law enforcement! Although we've already entered the realm of the 'Brave New World,' it's not too late to turn back."

I'm not so sure. DNA is collected from juveniles and stored in the database of twenty-nine states. Other states, as well as the U.S. government, have plans to establish, increase, or enlarge the collection and storage of these most intimate clues about who and what we are—genetic information that many of us are not even aware of ourselves.

The fact that DNA testing can help establish guilt with absolute certainty might allay public concern about false convictions.

Ricky McGinn was supposed to die by lethal injection on June 1, 2000, strapped to the same gurney in the same back room of the Huntsville, Texas, prison unit that Gary Graham fought like hell to avoid. Minutes before his scheduled execution, McGinn was granted a thirty-day stay on the recommendation of George W. Bush, who was then in California campaigning for president.

Some perceived the recommendation as a political maneuver by Bush handlers to flesh out his self-styled compassionate conservativism. Officially, though, the stay was granted so the lingering doubts about McGinn's guilt or innocence in the rape-murder of his twelve-year-old stepdaughter could be addressed. As tests began, we crossed our fingers, and they crossed theirs.

Meanwhile, what Amnesty International secretary general Pierre Sané has called a "conveyor belt of death" never slowed. Thomas Mason was executed as scheduled on June 12, 2000. John Burks was executed as scheduled two days later. The next day, they executed Paul Nuncio, as scheduled. Then the professionals who run the belt rested a week before their schedule listed the name of Gary Graham.

When sentenced to die in 1981, Gary Graham was seventeen years old. His nineteen years on death row transformed him into a self-proclaimed "freedom fighter." He changed his name to Shaka Sankofa. For all those years, like so many others, Graham maintained his innocence. People listened and believed.

It didn't matter. All the DNA tests in the world would not save him, for no evidence was left at the scene of the crime for which he was convicted. Gary's dying words indicted us all that night. "They are killing me! They are murdering another innocent Black man in Texas tonight!"

And yeah, they were—and they did—and they will again, until stopped. This is what the keepers do, in the name of us all.

Ricky McGinn said it wouldn't be an act of God or a presidential candidate that saved him, but science. As it turned out, that was just another lie that he played out as long as he could, buying himself a little more time, a few more days.

The DNA analysis concluded that McGinn had indeed raped and murdered twelve-year-old Stephanie Flanary after all. Texas rescheduled McGinn's execution for late September of 2000. By the time you read this, he will most likely be gone—and forgotten by all but a few.

Human rights advocates hope DNA testing will prevent the execution of innocent people, and that it will be a tool that will ultimately help to dismantle the death penalty altogether. It has raised serious questions about the credibility of our trial system, questions that have the potential to undermine support for capital punishment.

Yet the fact that DNA testing can help establish guilt with absolute certainty might allay public concern about false convictions, perhaps justifying continued or even expanded use of the death penalty. This unfortunate ricochet effect of Scheck's "magic bullet" serves as a chilling reminder that humanity's greatest breakthroughs are sometimes turned against its best intentions.

We who would abolish the death penalty must be tireless in our efforts to end this centuries-old chamber of horrors. The death penalty—for any reason, for anyone—has always been, is today, and shall forever be anathema to justice for individuals caught in its bloody machinery, and for any society that relies upon its inherent fraudulence to provide "safety" or enhance the common good.

The death penalty touches us all, tainting our lives with an ancient and evil corruption. The stench of what we do to one another under the cover of law or lawlessness will not go away simply by tinkering with the machinery in hopes that it will run a little more smoothly. We must stop the machine altogether and decide, with and for each other, that there is a better way.

I rejoice for A.B. Butler, Roy Criner, and their families. I pray that their lives will someday be whole again. Exoneration after more than a decade of being locked away on false charges is no more than a beginning. The state has erred terribly, admitted its errors, and released each of them—but no one can return the years that prison stole from each of their lives.

I mourn for Ricky McGinn and Gary Graham, for their families, and for those who died in the crimes for which each of them was executed. For Gary and Ricky, the suffering and punishment ended as the life seeped from their bodies on that gurney in the Walls Unit.

But the suffering of all those who put them there did not end. There is no closure to be had there—just a huge and gaping emptiness where human beings used to be.

12

The Unfairness of the Death Penalty Could Lead to Its Abolition

Eric Ruder

Eric Ruder is an editor of the International Socialist Review, *a quarterly Marxist journal.*

Both critics and supporters of the death penalty have grown increasingly concerned about the number of death row prisoners who have been found innocent of the crimes for which they were originally convicted. The likelihood that innocents could be executed has prompted several politicians and state legislatures to call for a suspension of capital punishment until the legal system can ensure its fair application. But the death penalty cannot be fixed; wrongful convictions and executions are part of a deeper problem in a criminal justice system that routinely discriminates on the basis of class and race. Those who oppose capital punishment should take advantage of the public's current concern about false convictions and biased sentencing. Public support for moratoria on executions coupled with dedicated grassroots activism could lead to the abolition of the death penalty altogether.

When Republican Illinois Gov. George Ryan announced a statewide moratorium on the death penalty on January 31, 2000, the debate over capital punishment was transformed. Ryan cited the fact that since 1976, Illinois has executed 12 people but released 13 from death row who were found to be innocent. He declared, "Until I can be sure that everyone sentenced to death in Illinois is truly guilty, until I can be sure with moral certainty that no innocent man or woman is facing lethal injection, no one will meet that fate." [Editor's note: In 2003, Ryan commuted Illinois' death sentences to life sentences without parole.]

Ryan's announcement is long overdue and represents a major victory for opponents of the death penalty in Illinois and around the country. For the first time in roughly two decades, the defenders of capital punishment have been thrown on the defensive. They are now forced to explain why their system is grinding up innocent people. Major newspapers across the country ran editorials against the death penalty in the wake of Ryan's decision, pointing out what death penalty abolitionists have been arguing for years. The *New York Times* wrote:

> Illinois is not the only state with a capital justice system so flawed that it cannot ensure that innocent people are spared. The solution ultimately is to end capital punishment, a system that cannot afford to mete out a single mistaken sentence.

The *Milwaukee Journal Sentinel* put it even more strongly:

> To support the death penalty is, in effect, to support the state-sanctioned killing of innocent people. Perhaps the taking of an innocent life every so often is a price some backers of the death penalty are willing to pay. But America should think hard about that cost. And Bill Clinton should suspend executions long enough to give the nation time to think.

In the two weeks after Gov. Ryan's decree, a flood of provisions questioning the use of the death penalty was introduced by mainstream politicians—another first in almost two decades. In response to an appeal by Sen. Russell Feingold (D-Wis.), President Clinton announced that he would consider a moratorium on the federal death penalty. Five U.S. senators urged Clinton to institute a moratorium until they could be sure that no innocent people sat on federal death row. Sen. Patrick Leahy (D-Vt.) proposed the Innocence Act of 2000, which would provide DNA testing for inmates who seek to prove that they did not commit the crime for which they were condemned. Sen. Feingold has since introduced a bill to eliminate the federal death penalty.

In 1999, 12 bills were introduced in 12 states, including Indiana and Missouri, to abolish the death penalty. In March 2000, the New Hampshire House voted 191 to 163 to abolish the death penalty—the first state to do so since executions resumed in 1976. Though New Hampshire's governor has threatened a veto—and no executions have been carried out in that state for 61 years—the vote is significant. Most sweeping of all has been the announcement by Rep. Jesse Jackson, Jr. (D-Ill.) that he would propose legislation in Congress calling for a seven-year moratorium on all executions in the U.S.

[The defenders of capital punishment] are now forced to explain why their system is grinding up innocent people.

In addition, the city councils of Philadelphia, San Francisco and Baltimore have passed resolutions calling on the governors of their respective states to follow Gov. Ryan's lead and implement moratoria.

Even individuals who have been at the heart of the death penalty system are expressing doubts. Former Pennsylvania Attorney General Ernie Preate, who had previously defended the constitutionality of Pennsylvania's death penalty before the U.S. Supreme Court, said in early March 2000, "I was once a constructor of this apparatus of death . . . [b]ut I can no longer support that which I helped create." These developments mark a fundamental shift from previous years, when the death penalty seemed beyond challenge. A real debate has opened up around the death penalty, and the possibility of halting executions is now on the agenda.

More executions, more horrors

Ironically, the very "success" of the death penalty—if measured in terms of the number of people killed by it—is what, in part, is fueling the rising doubts and opposition to its use. In 1999, 98 people were executed—the highest number in 50 years. In January 2000, three men were executed who had been juveniles when the crimes for which they were condemned were committed—compared to three juveniles executed in the rest of the *world* throughout the entire 1990s. In Texas, Gov. George W. Bush refused to grant clemency to Bettie Lou Beets, who was executed in late February 2000 for the murder of her violently abusive husband.

But nowhere are the cracks in the system of capital punishment more glaringly revealed than around the question of executing the innocent. Illinois has released 13 innocent men since 1976, and Florida has released 19 over the same period. To date, 87 people have been freed across the country. The fact that innocent people will be murdered by the state as the number of executions increases has forced a new debate on whether the death penalty should be used at all. It has also created the possibility for anti-death penalty activists to organize a real push for a moratorium nationally—and to use that momentum as a stepping-stone toward abolition.

Developments in Florida have put a spotlight on the number of innocent people facing execution, although in a completely perverse way. Unlike Gov. Ryan's decision in Illinois to temporarily halt executions, Florida legislators—despite the record number of innocent people released from death row there—overhauled the state's death penalty laws in early January to facilitate *quicker* executions. Their goal was to shorten the time spent on death row before execution from the current average of 11 years to five years. Brad Thomas, advisor to Florida Gov. Jeb Bush on the issue, told the *St. Petersburg Times,* "What I hope is that we become more like Texas. Bring in the witnesses, put them on a gurney, and let's rock and roll."

> A real debate has opened up around the death penalty, and the possibility of halting executions is now on the agenda.

No doubt, some number of the 19 people exonerated and released from Florida's death row would have been executed had these laws been enacted earlier. The average time innocent people spend on Florida's death row before they are exonerated is slightly more than seven years. One man—James Richardson—spent 21 years on death row before he was exonerated. Florida's mad rush to execute highlights the skewed demographics of judicial murder. According to the Death Penalty Information Center,

Southern states account for 500 of the 618 executions since 1976. Florida (41), Virginia (75) and Texas (209) alone account for 325 executions.

The increasing number of executions has also forced a public discussion of the dramatic inequalities built into the U.S. justice system—the inequalities of race and class—as well as the barbaric cruelty of executions and the corruption of the criminal justice system.

Race, class, and the death penalty

Together, the quickening pace of executions and stricter limits on state and federal appeals have exacerbated another appalling aspect of the death penalty: racism. The number of Blacks on death row grew to 43 percent in 1999 from 40 percent in the 1980s. More than half of the people on death row are Black or Latino, while these groups combined make up less than 23 percent of the U.S. population. Even more astonishing than the disproportionate number of minorities on death row is the racial disparity between cases involving Black and white murder victims. A study of Georgia's death row demonstrated that a Black person convicted of killing a white person is eleven times more likely to receive a death sentence than a white person convicted of killing a Black person. About 85 percent of the victims in death penalty cases are white, even though only 50 percent of murder victims are white.

Americans on average estimate that 10 percent of all people sentenced to death are innocent.

Of the 13 innocent people released from death row in Illinois, ten are Black or Latino. And several of them were not released because the system worked, as some supporters of the death penalty claim, but because students enrolled in a journalism class did investigative work that cleared them. Despite Gov. Ryan's moratorium, the Death Row 10—a group of Black men convicted and sentenced to death on the basis of "confessions" tortured out of them by police—still sit on death row. The police department's own review board, the Office of Professional Standards, has substantiated their allegations of police torture, yet members of the Death Row 10 still await execution. Reversing their convictions will require tremendous pressure because so many criminal justice officials—from police to prosecutors to judges—stand to have their careers destroyed if these cases are reopened.

Even more shocking than the scale of racial inequality revealed by the numbers are the stories that underlie these numbers. For example, according to Amnesty International:

> Michael Goggin, a former prosecutor for Cook County, Illinois, recently admitted that the District Attorney's office ran a contest to see which prosecutor could be the first to convict defendants whose weight totaled 4,000 pounds. Men and women upon conviction were marched into a room and weighed. Because most of the defendants were

black, the competition was known by local officials as "Niggers by the Pound."

Stories like these come to light against the backdrop of a general crisis in the criminal justice system. Police corruption scandals are breaking out all over. In Los Angeles, the biggest corruption scandal in decades has so far led to the release of more than 40 people who were wrongly convicted by crooked cops—and the number could climb much higher. In Philadelphia, thousands of cases have been reopened after the systematic planting of evidence by police was uncovered. And, in Chicago, four police were brought up on disciplinary charges for killing unarmed Black motorist LaTanya Haggerty in 1999; three were fired in March.

There is a widespread sense among ordinary people, especially among millions of Blacks and Latinos, that the police are given a free hand to systematically target minorities—to pull them over, search, beat and, in many cases, gun them down with impunity. The New York City cops' brutal murder of unarmed African immigrant Amadou Diallo in a hail of 41 bullets—19 of which struck him, most while he was already on the ground—and their subsequent acquittal is only one recent example. The prevalence of racial profiling—where police deliberately target minorities as criminal suspects simply because they are Black or Latino—has made "driving while Black" practically a household phrase.

"There are no millionaires sitting on death row. Can you honestly say to yourself, you're going to get equal justice under the law?" This insight—astoundingly—came from Republican State Rep. Anthony DiFruscia from New Hampshire during a debate over whether to abolish capital punishment. No one can dispute the truth of this statement—not even Republicans. Yet the poor, indigent and working-class men and women facing possible execution are forced to face well-funded prosecutorial teams with inexperienced, grossly underpaid lawyers.

The more people know about the death penalty, the less they support it.

Defendants in capital cases who cannot afford an attorney typically receive court-appointed attorneys who aren't given the financial resources to wage an adequate defense, who are incompetent or both. Even though weeks of intensive work are needed to prepare for a capital trial, Alabama limits reimbursement for capital cases to $2,000. In Texas, at least three attorneys assigned to defend the accused in capital trials have fallen asleep in the middle of the proceedings. Clinton's 1996 Anti-Terrorism and Effective Death Penalty Act eliminated funding for death penalty resource centers that helped death row inmates with trials and the appeals process, thereby exacerbating the problem of incompetent legal counsel. The Act also "restricts review in federal court by establishing tighter filing deadlines, limits the opportunity for evidentiary hearings, and allows only a single *habeas corpus* filing." The Act makes it nearly impossible to reverse mistakes made at trial—even if made by incompetent or sleeping lawyers. "The Constitution says that everyone's entitled to an attorney of their choice," Texas District Court Judge Doug Shaver argued. "But the Constitution does not say that the lawyer has to be awake."

International trend toward abolition

The United States stands alone among the most industrialized countries in increasing the number of executions. By 1980, 62 countries had abolished the death penalty in law or had ceased using it. By 1998, that number had climbed to 105. The U.S., China, Congo, Iran and Egypt are the countries that carried out the most executions in 1998. There is, therefore, an increasing contradiction between the frequent use of the death penalty in the U.S. and the verbal commitment to human rights by U.S. leaders.

Despite the hollowness of the U.S. claim to be a beacon of truth and light throughout the world, U.S. foreign policy depends on trumpeting itself as just such a "leader" in the area of human rights. But if other countries can point to the racism and inequality of the death penalty in the U.S., one of the chief ideological justifications for U.S. intervention around the world is undercut. Moreover, killing abroad—something the U.S. has perfected from Vietnam to Iraq . . . is the twin brother of killing at home. The challenge to one might be a challenge to the other.

Shift in public opinion

The Illinois moratorium and similar recent efforts have tapped into—and will in turn deepen—a shift in public opinion. This shift was already underway, but it has been largely hidden from view for the past few years. Diminishing support for the death penalty is no doubt the result of a growing distaste for the gore, racism and errors in its application that have become more visible as the rate of executions has grown. According to a recent Gallup poll, Americans on average estimate that 10 percent of all people sentenced to death are innocent—a remarkably high number.

While a majority across the country still supports the death penalty in general, this number has also declined. In the early 1950s, support for the death penalty was quite high at 68 percent. It then fell to its low point of 42 percent in 1966 as the civil rights movement began to shift the political climate. The high point in support for the death penalty came in 1994 at 80 percent. Since then, support has steadily declined to 66 percent—a drop of 14 percentage points. Support for the death penalty has not been this low since 1981. Perhaps more importantly, 28 percent of people today say that they are *opposed* to capital punishment—almost twice as many as the 16 percent who were opposed in 1994. The last time more people were opposed to capital punishment was in 1972, when 32 percent opposed it. In addition, support for the death penalty drops to about 50 percent nationally when the option of alternative sentences is offered. In some states, support drops even lower: California, 38 percent; New York, 38 percent; Michigan, 33 percent; New Jersey, 44 percent; Ohio, 31 percent; and Kentucky, 35 percent. In Ohio, 68 percent think that the likelihood of an innocent person being wrongly executed is either somewhat or very likely.

In those places where the death penalty is a subject of public discussion, the decline in support is even more marked than elsewhere in the country. In Texas, with its assembly-line killing machine, only a bare majority of 53 percent supports the death penalty if the death row inmate has "shown signs of turning his or her life around." Death penalty support dropped significantly in Texas after the 1998 execution of Karla Faye Tucker. In Illinois, 81 percent of residents support Gov. Ryan's decision to call for a moratorium.

There is no way to fix the death penalty.

Not surprisingly, Philadelphia, San Francisco and Baltimore—the three largest cities that have passed resolutions in favor of a moratorium—have been the site of numerous anti-death penalty protests. Ten thousand people gathered in Philadelphia in 1999 to demand a new trial for Mumia Abu-Jamal, America's most visible death row inmate [Abu-Jamal's death sentence was overturned in 2001. He is now serving a life sentence for his murder conviction.] In Illinois, there have been dozens of demonstrations against the death penalty, successful efforts by journalism students to exonerate wrongly convicted death row inmates and protests about the Death Row 10. Five hundred people demonstrated in Chicago for a moratorium after Anthony Porter became the tenth man released from Illinois' death row. Porter and Darby Tillis, another of the former death row inmates released in Illinois, spoke at the demonstration.

This trend confirms something that anti-death penalty activists have long known: The more people know about the death penalty, the less they support it. This dynamic can only be helped by recent films *The Green Mile, The Hurricane* and *True Crime,* and recent episodes of popular TV shows *The Practice* and *The West Wing.* Benetton's "We, On Death Row" advertising campaign also powerfully depicts all of the problems with the death penalty. The popularity of Rage Against the Machine's CD, *The Battle of Los Angeles,* whose lyrics challenge racism and the death penalty, also reflects a growing mood among young people against the injustice system.

The anti-death penalty position will gain a wider audience as more individual politicians cave in to the pressure generated by closer scrutiny of the death rows in their states. As the stories of racism and innocence on death row get a broader hearing, death penalty supporters will have to work harder to find convincing justifications for capital punishment. And their options are increasingly limited. The pro-death camp has had to abandon, for example, the argument that the death penalty is needed to deter crime—because no credible study has been able to prove this. Some studies even suggest that the death penalty has a "brutalizing" effect on society, which degrades the sanctity of human life. As evidence for this, a recent article in the *Arizona Star* cited a 1997 study that calculated the murder rate in the 38 states with capital punishment at 6.6 per 100,000. In the 12 other states and the District of Columbia, it was 3.5. What is left to bolster the pro-death penalty case is vengeance and retribution for the sake of the victims' surviving family members, a comparatively ugly and sadistic justification that many—including many victims' family members—are repulsed by.

Building a movement from below

For the first time in decades, a significant fissure in the right-wing consensus around "tough on crime" policies has emerged. The issue of crime first played a major role in mainstream national politics during Richard Nixon's successful campaign for president in 1968. In an effort to find a way to appeal to racist voters without the open use of racist terms, Nixon began to deploy the rhetoric of "law and order" against the supposed "lawlessness" of the civil rights movement. Nixon wrote, for example, that America was "the most lawless and violent [nation] in the history of free peoples," which he blamed on the "growing tolerance of lawlessness" by civil rights organizations and "the increasing public acceptance of civil disobedience." He attacked his Democratic opponent, Vice President Hubert Humphrey, for showing "permissiveness toward the lawless" because Humphrey said, "For every jail Mr. Nixon wants to build, I'd like to build a house for a family."

Over the years, the Democratic Party—which had succeeded in the past by forging an unholy alliance between Southern "Dixiecrats" and Northern liberals—developed a strategy to "out-Republican" the Republicans on the issue of crime. The Democratic Leadership Council (DLC), headed by none other than then-Arkansas Gov. Bill Clinton, was the vehicle built within the Democratic Party to drive it to the right. The DLC strategy was simple: Win over the Democrats who voted for Reagan.

The "line 'em up and kill 'em" approach to the death penalty is for the first time reeling from its own failures.

In particular, Clinton rode his "tough on crime" credentials into the White House in 1992. Under the Clinton administration, the number of federal crimes punishable by death increased from two to 60. Former Attorney General Janet Reno sought the death penalty on an unprecedented scale. Clinton's success at outflanking Republicans on the crime issue has been emulated by many throughout the Democratic Party. California Gov. Gray Davis beat Republican Attorney General Dan Lungren in 1998 in part by praising the criminal justice practices of the dictatorship in Singapore, which made international headlines after its brutal caning of an American teenager arrested for painting graffiti. "I think Singapore is a good starting point in terms of law and order," Davis said. "I think there ought to be clear rules. You can't punish people enough as far as I'm concerned." After the debate, Davis continued. "We're just talking about violent crime and the death penalty. I think Singapore has very clear rules. They don't fool around. There's virtually no crime. If you don't like it, get on a plane and go someplace else."

The drum of law-and-order politics that has been steadily beaten by both parties for more than two decades now has had predictable effects: a relentless drive to build prisons, prosecute, incarcerate and execute. In February 2000, the U.S. incarcerated its two millionth person—making it the largest jailer in the world, responsible for locking up fully 25 percent of the world's prison population. For these reasons, Gov. Ryan's decision to impose a moratorium in Illinois is highly significant. The pressure of activists and the intolerable spectacle of a capital punishment machine that reluctantly releases as many innocents from its clutches as it executes combined to force a pro-death penalty Republican to impose the first moratorium in the country. Furthermore, Gov. Ryan headed up the Illinois presidential campaign of Texas Gov. George W. Bush—who turned the office of governor into an executioner's chamber, overseeing more than 120 executions during his term.

Gov. Ryan's ultimate goal is not to abolish the death penalty, but to save it from its credibility crisis in Illinois. However, the crisis has created a dynamic that Gov. Ryan may not be able to control. While he has established a commission to study Illinois' death row and "fix" the system, our side can use the time to organize and demonstrate that there is no way to fix the death penalty.

Now that the climate has begun to shift, there is a renewed energy to fight the death penalty on the part of different organizations that have long faced a seemingly uphill battle. Amnesty International, for example, which has a general policy of not allowing its various national sections to address domestic matters, has in recent years made an exception in the case of the U.S. death penalty. . . .

In 2000, the Campaign to End the Death Penalty drafted an "Open Letter to President Clinton and Members of Congress," which calls on politicians to support Rep. Jackson's moratorium bill. By encouraging various well-known individuals—such as Rev. Jesse Jackson, Sr., and his Rainbow/PUSH Coalition; actors Susan Sarandon and Tim Robbins; former Illinois death row prisoners Anthony Porter, Darby Tillis and Perry Cobb; American Bar Association head Ron Tabak; Amnesty International's Sam Jordan; and Bianca Jagger—to sign the "Open Letter," the moratorium movement can develop a more visible national presence. . . .

The shift among some politicians who are now willing to do something about capital punishment is a welcome change, and one abolitionists should take advantage of. We can work with individual Democratic politicians who oppose capital punishment in order to help publicize and broaden the level of participation in the struggle for a moratorium. But we shouldn't lose sight of the fact that the Democratic Party has a pro-death penalty platform. . . . Clinton pulled back from considering a federal moratorium after he floated a trial balloon on the issue. Instead, he reaffirmed his support for capital punishment, but praised Gov. Ryan, calling on governors to examine the death penalty in their states. This allowed Clinton to put a spotlight on the gruesome records of Republicans like George W. Bush and his brother, Florida Gov. Jeb Bush—without having to change his own stance. . . .

Abolition last time

In 1972, the U.S. Supreme Court ruled that the death penalty violated the Eighth Amendment against "cruel and unusual punishment" and the Fourteenth Amendment guaranteeing equal protection under the law. Crucially, the decision focused on the arbitrary, racist and capricious way that capital punishment was implemented, but the Court did not rule that capital punishment itself was unconstitutional. While this was a welcome decision in any case, it came as a shock. Much like Gov. Ryan's decision to declare a moratorium in Illinois, anti-death penalty activists and lawyers were surprised by the decision. Two liberal justices had recently retired and were replaced by appointees of Republican President Richard Nixon.

Now is the time to mobilize and use the fight for a moratorium as a stepping-stone in the fight for total abolition.

The 1972 victory came largely as an indirect product of the civil rights movement. On the one hand, the courts had been forced to give more credence to the problem of discrimination in society as a whole and to the issue of civil rights and civil liberties in the criminal justice system in particular. On the other hand, public opinion had shifted against the death penalty over the previous 10 years as the civil rights movement succeeded in generalizing an awareness of social problems and tens of thousands were galvanized into political activism.

But as far as the death penalty itself was concerned, only one national anti-death penalty organization existed in the early 1970s—and it was largely dormant. The challenge to the death penalty had been mostly relegated to a legal fight waged by lawyers from the National Association for the Advancement of Colored People Legal Defense Fund (LDF). The LDF had taken up the issue of the death penalty because it was so frequently sought against Black defendants who had been accused of rape in the South. Although the LDF succeeded in 1972, there was a price for this legalistic approach. [According to Herbert Haines, author of *Against Capital Punishment*,] "Through most of the moratorium period [1972–76], the majority of citizens and their elected officials had remained rather passive about the issue." In fact, some "elected officials" were worse than passive. In the effort to find a way to appeal to racist voters, politicians began to deploy Nixon's law-and-order strategy. So despite the declaration by the U.S. Supreme Court of a moratorium on all executions in the U.S., support for the death penalty climbed from 50 percent to 66 percent of all Americans between 1972 and 1976.

Abolition this time

This time around, a number of factors put us in a favorable position to challenge the death penalty.

For one, a shift in public opinion away from the death penalty is already underway—even before the development of a mass movement like the civil rights movement has dramatically shifted the general political climate. This is due to a number of factors already covered: horror at the growing number of executions, a growing awareness of racism and brutality throughout the criminal justice system and the class inequality that underlies the death penalty.

The moratorium in Illinois has given enormous credibility to anti-death penalty activists who have long argued that the death penalty kills innocent people. This victory was won in large part by the efforts of activists who would not allow the system's obvious failings to be forgotten as easily as death penalty supporters would have liked. Now, this victory stands as a model to be emulated elsewhere. Even with relatively small numbers of activists, the climate is one in which it may be possible to abolish the death penalty—much as the women's rights movement won abortion rights in the early 1970s. Though the largest abortion rights demonstration in the country was no more than 10,000 people, there were hundreds of smaller protests across the country. Together, these pushed the U.S. Supreme Court to rule in favor of a woman's right to choose in 1973.

Today, anti-death penalty activists have an opportunity to repeat this example. And while the participation of high-profile celebrities and politicians is welcome, abolishing the death penalty will require far more: the building of an active, grassroots movement.

The "line 'em up and kill 'em" approach to the death penalty is for the first time reeling from its own failures. The criminal justice system cannot justify a death penalty that frees as many people as it kills. Now is the time to mobilize and use the fight for a moratorium as a stepping-stone in the fight for total abolition. Whether or not the death penalty is scrapped in the U.S. will depend on the organized action of thousands of people who are determined to win.

13

Abolitionists' Arguments Should Focus on Morality Rather than Fairness

R. Emmett Tyrrell Jr.

R. Emmett Tyrrell Jr. is editor in chief of the American Spectator, *a conservative journal of opinion.*

The argument that capital punishment should be abolished because it is discriminatory and inconsistently applied is an evasive form of false reasoning. There is no evidence that innocents have been executed or that capital punishment is less fair than any other enforced laws and sentences. The death penalty should be abolished because it kills and because it is immoral—not because it is unfair.

When the state of Texas, governed by putative Republican presidential candidate Governor George W. Bush, executed Gary Graham for murder, I found myself in unlikely company. There I was, opposing the death penalty and pleading clemency for a very evil man in the company of the celebrity humanitarians Bianca Jagger, the Reverend Jesse Jackson and the Reverend Al Sharpton.

This was not particularly comforting. Historical developments over the last decade have made irrefutable what ratiocination had earlier made clear: to wit, on public issues this fabulous trinity is almost always wrong. How could they now be right? Well, they were not right—at least, not completely right. Their reasoning was flawed and their arguments shoddy. Still, the conclusion that we had come to share was correct. Graham should not have been executed by the state. As to what should be done with Graham, the trinity remains silent. Possibly Bianca favours aerobics and cosmetic surgery. Probably the Reverends recommend that he go on a lecture tour. I remember the Reverend Jackson suggesting, after O.J. Simpson's murder trial, that he become a national spokesman for battered women—no joke!

As for me, I would have Graham locked away for life. That is my al-

R. Emmett Tyrrell Jr., "The Abolitionist's Song," *The Spectator*, vol. 285, July 1, 2000, pp. 18–19.

ternative to capital punishment. Given the benefit of clergy and of counsel, an ample library and solitary reflection, even a murderer such as Graham might attain contrition for his cruelty. Graham's crimes include shootings, robberies and rapes, cruelties for which restitution is realistically impossible. However, had he lived he might have been able to make peace with his Maker and to bear witness to the evil of his crimes. As it was, he died a hero to those who find something fascinating, perhaps even noble, about criminals.

The popular arguments for sparing the likes of Graham no longer stress that capital punishment is an evil or question the state's right to execute. Now the popular argument is that capital punishment kills innocent people, that blacks are sentenced to death disproportionately, and that capital punishment is inconsistently applied. All are false arguments. When the public sees through these sophistries it will grow even more impatient with the anti-capital-punishment position.

Why end executions?

The most compelling case for ending state executions is that, though the state has a right to defend its citizenry, capital punishment merely silences life. It neither dramatises the horror of crime nor speaks out for life. It adds to the increasing anger and morbidness in society. America in its entertainments, its public ethics and its socially accepted misbehaviour, is increasingly brutal. A growing sector of its culture is, indeed, entoiled with death.

Ever since the Supreme Court's 1976 decision reinstating the death penalty (*Gregg v. Georgia*) support for it has waxed and waned; so has the ardour of the death penalty's opponents, who tend to be numbered among the country's elites and viewed sceptically by the country's majority (interestingly, the elites of most Western countries oppose the death penalty while most ordinary citizens favour it). In the 1970s public support for capital punishment was rising steadily from its post-second world war low. It continued to rise in the 1980s. By 1994 approval reached a colossal 80 per cent, only to recede to 66 per cent in the most recent Gallup poll. Meanwhile the elites' opposition has also changed.

> *The most compelling case for ending state executions is that . . . capital punishment merely silences life.*

In 1992 Governor Bill Clinton, reading the polls with his usual astuteness, left the presidential campaign trail temporarily, returning to Arkansas to preside over his state's execution of one Rickey Ray Rector, who, incidentally, was so mentally impaired that he left for his execution chamber promising cell guards that he would finish his dessert after the proceedings were over. My colleagues, the celebrity humanitarians, will for their labours on Graham's behalf have no influence on capital punishment's popularity. Most likely, they will increase the public's cynicism about the way elites exploit the issue. Certainly their favoured arguments are exploitative, relying as they do on public ignorance.

The trendiest of their arguments is that innocents are being executed owing to errors made by lawyers, judges and jurors. Actually, not one of the over 600 convicted murderers executed since 1976 has subsequently been proven innocent. Not even the popular report from which this argument has gained momentum identifies an innocent victim of capital punishment. Rather, the report claims that there is a 68 per cent 'error rate' in capital cases. The errors referred to involve clerical error, errors owing to changing standards of due process and other legal mistakes. At the end of this due-process marathon, convicted murderers have been set free, but no innocent person has been executed. Viewed from a different perspective, one could conclude that the due process accorded capital trials is so exacting that American courts err on the side of liberality rather than severity.

More sophistry

The next most popular argument—that blacks are disproportionately put to death—is also sophistry. Unfortunately, blacks commit a disproportionate number of crimes (usually against other blacks). The crimes are disproportionately more brutal, and more likely to be capital offences. As for the argument that capital punishment is enforced inconsistently, there is inconsistency in the enforcement of many laws. The fact remains that innocent lives have not been lost to public execution in the United States.

If Americans want to reduce the loss of innocent lives, they might look to the lives that are lost owing to slipshod enforcement of parole and probation. According to a recent justice department report, during a 17-month period beginning in 1995 criminals released on parole and probation and still 'under supervision' committed an astounding 13,200 murders. They also were responsible for some 200,000 other violent crimes.

And that brings me to the heart of my case against the death penalty, a case that I think many who now favour the death penalty will find persuasive. To be sure, a government has a duty to defend its citizens against danger, but that was accomplished once Gary Graham was behind bars. Killing him merely made him a star in our witless celebrity culture. Once executed he has no chance to acknowledge his wrongs. Society has less chance to reflect on the brutality of such a man's life of crime. There may once have been a day when capital punishment was illustrative of condign retribution, but not in our day.

In a society that exploits coarseness and violence in its entertainments, even in its advertisements, such niceties as retribution are lost. American society offers up vast areas of violence—admittedly, usually simulated—for the amusement of sports fans, film-goers, popular-music idiots. Even many television advertisements feature transmogrifications of the average Joe screeching off in some fanciful vehicle or flying through a window in pursuit of some flashy product: a new beer! an invincible deodorant! In its hype and its pervasive materialism, all boomed with an adolescent cynicism, America does encourage a culture not about life and ebullience but about death and the repugnant. An end to capital punishment would signal a respect for life and an acknowledgment of evil. Right, Bianca?

Organizations to Contact

The editors have compiled the following list of organizations concerned with the issues debated in this book. The descriptions are derived from materials provided by the organizations. All have publications or information available for interested readers. The list was compiled on the date of publication of the present volume; the information provided here may change. Be aware that many organizations take several weeks or longer to respond to inquiries, so allow as much time as possible.

American Civil Liberties Union (ACLU)
Capital Punishment Project
125 Broad St., 18th Floor, New York, NY 10004
(212) 549-2500 • fax: (212) 549-2646
website: www.aclu.org

The project is dedicated to abolishing the death penalty. The ACLU believes that capital punishment violates the Constitution's ban on cruel and unusual punishment as well as the requirements of due process and equal protection under the law. It publishes and distributes numerous books and pamphlets, including *The Case Against the Death Penalty* and *Frequently Asked Questions Concerning the Writ of Habeas Corpus and the Death Penalty.*

Amnesty International USA (AI)
322 Eighth Ave., New York, NY 10001
(212) 807-8400 • fax: (212) 627-1451
website: www.amnesty-usa.org

Amnesty International is an independent worldwide movement working impartially for the release of all prisoners of conscience, fair and prompt trials for political prisoners, and an end to torture and executions. AI is funded by donations from its members and supporters throughout the world. AI has published several books and reports, including *Fatal Flaws: Innocence and the Death Penalty.*

Canadian Coalition Against the Death Penalty (CCADP)
PO Box 38104, 550 Eglinton Ave. W, Toronto, ON M5N 3A8 CANADA
(416) 693-9112 • fax: (416) 686-1630
e-mail: ccadp@home.com • website: www.ccadp.org

CCADP is a not-for-profit international human rights organization dedicated to educating the public on alternatives to the death penalty worldwide and to providing emotional and practical support to death row inmates, their families, and the families of murder victims. The coalition releases pamphlets and periodic press releases, and its website includes a student resource center providing research information on capital punishment.

Death Penalty Focus of California
74 New Montgomery, Suite 250, San Francisco, CA 94105
(415) 243-0143 • fax: (415) 243-0994
e-mail: info@deathpenalty.org • website: www.deathpenalty.org

Death Penalty Focus of California is a nonprofit organization dedicated to the abolition of capital punishment through grassroots organization, research, and the dissemination of information about the death penalty and its alternatives. It publishes the quarterly newsletter *The Sentry.*

Death Penalty Information Center (DPIC)
1606 20th St. NW, 2nd Floor, Washington, DC 20009
(202) 347-2531
website: www.essential.org/dpic

DPIC conducts research into public opinion on the death penalty. The center believes capital punishment is discriminatory and excessively costly and that it may result in the execution of innocent persons. It publishes numerous reports, such as *Millions Misspent: What Politicians Don't Say About the High Costs of the Death Penalty, Innocence and the Death Penalty: Assessing the Danger of Mistaken Executions,* and *With Justice for Few: The Growing Crisis in Death Penalty Representation.*

Justice Fellowship (JF)
PO Box 16069, Washington, DC 20041-6069
(703) 904-7312 • fax: (703) 478-9679
website: www.justicefellowship.org

This Christian organization bases its work for reform of the justice system on the concept of victim-offender reconciliation. It does not take a position on the death penalty, but it publishes the pamphlet *Capital Punishment: A Call to Dialogue.*

Justice for All (JFA)
PO Box 55159, Houston, TX 77255
(713) 935-9300 • fax: (713) 935-9301
e-mail: jfanet@msn.com • website: www.jfa.net

Justice for All is a not-for-profit criminal justice reform organization that supports the death penalty. Its activities include circulating online petitions to keep violent offenders from being paroled early and publishing the monthly newsletter *The Voice of Justice.*

Lamp of Hope Project
PO Box 305, League City, TX 77574-0305
e-mail: ksebung@c-com.net • website: www.lampofhope.org

The project was established and is run primarily by Texas death row inmates. It works for victim-offender reconciliation and for the protection of the civil rights of prisoners, particularly the right of habeas corpus appeal. It publishes and distributes the periodic *Texas Death Row Journal.*

Lincoln Institute for Research and Education
1001 Connecticut Ave. NW, Washington, DC 20036
(202) 223-5112

The institute is a conservative think tank that studies public policy issues affecting the lives of black Americans, including the issue of the death penalty, which it favors. It publishes the quarterly *Lincoln Review.*

National Coalition to Abolish the Death Penalty (NCADP)
1436 U St. NW, Suite 104, Washington, DC 20009
(202) 387-3890 • fax: (202) 387-5590
e-mail: info@ncadp • website: www.ncadp.org

The National Coalition to Abolish the Death Penalty is a collection of more than 115 groups working together to stop executions in the United States. The organization compiles statistics on the death penalty. To further its goal, the coalition publishes *Legislative Action to Abolish the Death Penalty*, information packets, pamphlets, and research materials.

National Criminal Justice Reference Service (NCJRS)
U.S. Department of Justice
PO Box 6000, Rockville, MD 20849-6000
(301) 519-5500 • (800) 851-3420 • fax: (301) 519-5212
e-mail: askncjrs@ncjrs.org • website: www.ncjrs.org

The National Criminal Justice Reference Service is one of the most extensive sources of information on criminal and juvenile justice in the world. For a nominal fee, this clearinghouse provides topical searches and reading lists on many areas of criminal justice, including the death penalty. It publishes an annual report on capital punishment.

Bibliography

Books

Mumia Abu-Jamal	*All Things Censored.* New York: Seven Stories Press, 2000.
Amnesty International	*On the Wrong Side of History: Children and the Death Penalty in the USA.* New York: Amnesty International USA, 1998.
Stuart Banner	*The Death Penalty: An American History.* Cambridge, MA: Harvard University Press, 2002.
Hugo Adam Bedau, ed.	*The Death Penalty in America.* New York: Oxford University Press, 1998.
Walter Berns	*For Capital Punishment.* Lanham, MD: University Press of America, 2000.
David Crump and George Jacobs	*A Capital Case in America: How Today's Justice System Handles Death Penalty Cases, from Crime Scene to Ultimate Execution of Sentence.* Durham, NC: Carolina Academic Press, 2000.
Shirley Dicks	*Death Row: Interviews with Inmates, Their Families and Opponents of Capital Punishment.* New York: iUniverse.com, 2001.
David Dow and Mark Dow, eds.	*The Machinery of Death: The Reality of America's Death Penalty Regime.* New York: Routledge, 2002.
John F. Galliher et al.	*America Without the Death Penalty: States Leading the Way.* Boston: Northeastern University Press, 2002.
L. Kay Gillespie	*Executions and the Execution Process: Questions and Answers.* Boston: Allyn and Bacon, 2002.
James S. Hirsch	*Hurricane: The Miraculous Journey of Rubin Carter.* Waterville, ME: Thorndike Press, 2000.
Jesse L. Jackson Sr., Jesse L. Jackson Jr., and Bruce Shapiro	*Legal Lynching: The Death Penalty and America's Future.* New York: New Press, 2001.
Robert J. Lifton	*Who Owns Death? Capital Punishment, the American Conscience, and the End of Executions.* New York: Perennial, 2002.
Michael Mello	*Deathwork: Defending the Condemned.* Minneapolis: University of Minnesota Press, 2002.
Louis P. Pojman and Jeffrey Reiman	*The Death Penalty: For and Against.* Lanham, MD: Rowman & Littlefield, 1998.

Austin Sarat   *When the State Kills: Capital Punishment and the American Condition.* Princeton, NJ: Princeton University Press, 2002.

Tom Streissguth   *The Death Penalty: Debating Capital Punishment.* Berkeley Heights, NJ: Enslow, 2002.

Periodicals

Alan Berlow   "The Broken Machinery of Death," *American Prospect,* July 30, 2001.

Walter Berns and   "Why the Death Penalty Is Fair," *Wall Street Journal,*
Joseph Bessette   January 9, 1998.

Alexander Cockburn   "Hate Versus Death," *Nation,* March 12, 2001.

Richard Cohen   "One Fatal Mistake Not Made," *Washington Post,* February 15, 2001.

Ann Coulter   "O.J. Was 'Proved Innocent,' Too," *Human Events,* June 20, 2000.

Catherine Cowan   "States Revisit the Death Penalty," *State Government News,* May 2001.

Gregg Easterbrook   "The Myth of Fingerprints: DNA and the End of Innocence," *New Republic,* July 31, 2000.

Don Feder   "It's Hard to Pardon the Excuses Given by Death-Penalty Opponents," *Insight on the News,* July 16, 2001.

Allan Fotheringham   "Death Penalty Insanity," *Maclean's,* March 19, 2001.

Joshua Green   "Second Thoughts on the Death Penalty," *American Prospect,* March 27, 2000.

Linda Greenhouse   "Citing 'National Consensus,' Justices Bar Death Penalty for Retarded Defendants," *New York Times,* June 21, 2002.

Jennifer L. Harry   "Death Penalty Disquiet Stirs Nation," *Corrections Today,* December 2000.

Cathleen C.   "Keep Inmates' IQs Out of Death Penalty Decisions,"
Herasimchuk   *Houston Chronicle,* May 21, 1999.

Jeff Jacoby   "The Abolitionists' Cop-Out," *Boston Globe,* June 8, 2000.

Nathan Koppel   "Selective Execution," *American Lawyer,* September 2001.

Patrick O'Neill   "Moratorium Leader Sees Hope for End of Death Penalty," *National Catholic Reporter,* January 19, 2001.

John O'Sullivan   "A Logical and Just Practice," *National Review,* July 17, 2000.

Progressive   "The Case Against the Death Penalty," February 2000.

Anna Quindlen   "The Call from the Governor," *Newsweek,* June 19, 2000.

Michael B. Ross   "Don't Execute Mentally Disturbed Killers," *Humanist,* January 1999.

William Saleton	"TRB from Washington: Life Time," *New Republic*, June 19, 2000.
Bruce Shapiro	"Rethinking the Death Penalty: Politicians and Courts Are Taking Their Cues from Growing Public Opposition," *Nation*, July 22, 2002.
Joseph B. Shapiro	"The Wrong Men on Death Row," *U.S. News & World Report*, November 9, 1998.
Andrew Stephen	"Where Race Puts You on Death Row," *New Statesman* (1996), March 5, 1999.
Ronald J. Tabak	"Racial Discrimination in the Death Penalty," *Human Rights*, Summer 1999.
Stuart Taylor Jr.	"The Death Penalty: To Err Is Human," *National Journal*, February 12, 2000.
Charles Whitaker	"The Death Penalty Debate: Are We Killing Innocent Black Men?" *Ebony*, May 1999.
James Q. Wilson	"What Death-Penalty Errors?" *New York Times*, July 10, 2000.

Index